JANE DOW
who comes

psychology and contemporary feminism—a philosophy she describes as essentially centred around the fundamental belief in non-aggressive means of solving problems.

In 1985 she incorporated The Change Agency, a management consultancy specialising in training for the corporate world. These days her client list reads like a Who's Who of public and private sector organisations in Australia.

Most of Jane's research and teachings over the years have centred around issues of changing interpersonal communication habits to both empower the individual as well as disturb and ultimately change what she sees as an oppressive patriarchal society. Jane calls this altered practice of communication 'power-with'.

Since 1988 Jane has developed and conducted leading-edge Human Resource Development to promote culture change within organisational life. She also lectures at the Queensland University of Technology in the Faculty of Business, where she encourages students to raise their critical consciousness regarding issues of power within relationships and in the workplace.

Jane's position is that many of the tenets of radical feminism are congruent with the changes needed in workplace reform, improved interpersonal relationships, and for planetary survival. For over ten years she has believed that learned interpersonal habits in communication can either perpetuate more of the same win–lose dynamics in relationships, or empower us to a new way of communicating that involves truly collaborative techniques and results in not only a different future, but a future where **difference** is celebrated.

FINDING YOUR VOICE

Reclaiming personal power through communication

Jane Downing

ALLEN & UNWIN

Because of May Downing (1902–94)
and Jane Collings (1899–1959).
While my grandmothers' lives had purpose that is not necessarily
mine, I am grateful to inherit their tradition of fierceness. Each
generation of women give birth to their own meanings. I am a
warrior. The fierce purpose of my life is change.

© Jane Downing, 1995

This book is copyright under the Berne Convention.
No reproduction without permission. All rights reserved.

First published in 1995 by
Allen & Unwin Pty Ltd
9 Atchison Street
St Leonards, NSW 2065 Australia

National Library of Australia
Cataloguing-in-Publication entry:

Downing, Jane, 1958– .
  Finding your voice: reclaiming personal power
  through communication.

  Includes index.
  ISBN 1 86373 829 0.

  1. Interpersonal communication. 2. Interpersonal relations.
  3. Assertiveness training. 4. Self-actualization
  (Psychology). 5. Self-help techniques. I. Title.

302.2

Set in 11/13 pt Goudy by DOCUPRO, Sydney
Printed by SRM Production Services Sdn Bhd, Malaysia

10 9 8 7 6 5 4 3 2 1

Contents

302.2
Downing)

CONTENTS

Figures

Author's Note

THIS IS A practical 'how to' guide for the popular area of **interpersonal communication skills**. It is also different. I treat this material as I teach it, in a way that most authors do not.

I believe how we speak reflects the habits of an oppressive culture—a society of people who have been socialised into thinking and acting in win–lose ways. I call this **'power-over'**. This book is an attempt to link the skills of assertion to ways of living that reclaim 'power-within' self and thereby allow for relationships of **'power-with'** others.

Since I started to speak about the potential of our communication skills to either maintain or disturb the status quo of an unjust society, I have received enthusiastic praise and support from many of my course participants and clients. It seems that my habit of situating 'assertion' within a social justice framework easily appeals to some people. I find increasing numbers of us are tremendously attracted to exploring ways of sharing 'power' with each other.

I have also felt the backlash of anger from others who may be afraid of my views about choices in how we relate to others, and the consequences of these choices. Some of the apparently 'successful' people and professionals I teach are quite disturbed by the concept that 'the way things are' may really be part of an ideological distortion that does not serve the interests of all equitably. It is not easy to accept information which directly opposes beliefs we have held for a long time. Nevertheless, I believe it is critical that each of us reassess how we are relating to ourselves and others and make changes that are less destructive to all people and perhaps even the planet.

I have come to believe that interpersonal communication skills are not just techniques for empowering the individual in relationships with others. Our habits of speaking and listening come from someplace and lead to somewhere. I have written this book for myself and for others who are waking up from the largely unconscious, middle-class, mainstream life which we may have traded for an absence of pain. I believe that more and more of us are becoming 'conscious' and realising the lies, games and soul-withering consequences of accepting and thereby supporting the status quo of our culture.

This discourse is offered to you in the spirit of sharing skills and ideas which are largely the opposite of conventions that I have come to believe are narrow and hurt many of us.

Acknowledgments

AFTER MANY YEARS of thinking, writing and teaching in the area of personal growth, communications and self-esteem I have no doubt developed hybrid forms of the ideas and works of some other people. My sources are eclectic, and increasingly, I am less clear about where one person's views end and mine begin. I would like to credit with real gratitude some of the people who I recognise as having helped and inspired me.

In the area of communication skills I was taught by a man who excited my original interest in the use/abuse of power. I appreciated the time with you Ian Lynagh. I recall being impressed with and influenced by a course and a book called 'ETW'—*Effectiveness Training for Women* by Linda Evans. For years I recommended it above all others ('in the absence of the one I would write myself one day'). In management training, *Management of Organisational Behaviour* written by Paul Hersey and Ken Blanchard, has remained the favourite model of leadership effectiveness for the managers who are my course participants.

For pure inspiration there was always the writings of Adrienne Rich, for consciousness pricking, the words and music of Judy Small and for spiritual uplift one person stands out as 'magic' in marrying politics with the spirit—Starhawk.

To Janet, love, friend and constant supporter—you remain my hero. To Trish who schedules herself 'on' so I can take time off—thank you my friend.

To Jenny the 'colourful cushion' of belief in me and champion of every step I take, I am truly grateful for your much needed reframing of my slumps and doubts. And to Katherine (of the last-minute push)—you are very easy to trust.

To all the thousands of learners and participants in my courses who have told me 'I really needed this stuff'—thanks. Your hunger inspires me, particularly on the zillionth day of teaching 'I statements'. All teachers really need is to believe that what we do can actually make a difference.

Preface

FOR AROUND TEN years I have been designing and conducting training programs for industry, government and community groups. The majority of my courses are in managerial effectiveness, teamwork, and are, lately, commonly entitled 'culture change'. All courses incorporate significant amounts of information and skills work in interpersonal communication skills.

For the first few years of my practice the topic of 'people skills' was not seen as important or necessary enough to constitute a course in its own right. Most employers saw 'assertion' and 'listening' as acceptable only if they were part of a more 'relevant' course in supervisory development or customer service. My perspective was that communication skills were just about the most important part of any program. In the work I do, this has remained my emphasis.

For various reasons, the choices that I (and then later my colleagues and I) made resulted in our management consultancy offering only in-house courses. Very rarely have we conducted a 'public' course. It was always my intention to write a book that would be some kind of a 'hitchhiker's guide' for people who either didn't want to or couldn't find or afford a training program such as the ones I conduct. It took me nearly nine years to find what I needed in both time and motivation to write this book.

I have always truly believed that win–win (power-with) interpersonal habits are a significant tool of empowerment at the personal level. In recent years I have embraced the possibility of these same skills being a significant part of what is needed to disturb and provoke the politics of a society marked by win–lose oppressive power dynamics. These days, the people I teach are introduced to how the concepts of *power-over* and *power-with* might provide insight into how people in our culture communicate.

Happily for me, my interest in creating culture change away from *power-over* towards co-operative sharing of power to solve problems has coincided with the shifts occurring in organisational development and human resource development. In recent years, the emphasis in organisational change and workplace reform has encouraged me to connect the philosophy of my social justice beliefs with the tenets of organisational change and development.

My own experience tells me that the sort of people who want or need to learn the skills of *power-with* interpersonal communication tend to be anyone and come from just about anywhere. These skills are much sought after by business men and women—including those who, in the past, have assumed that win–win communication is probably something of a 'soft option extra'. Parents are very interested in these skills, so too are teachers attempting to influence their learners, as are leaders needing to manage the performance of their staff. Just about anybody who needs to solve problems, make decisions and plan, or whose daily work involves negotiation, counselling or providing a service to a client, may wish to change the way that they relate to themselves or other people.

I have heard it said that there are many reasons for writing a book, not the least of which often involves us writing what it is we need to know about ourselves. Certainly, I found that as the book unfolded it changed from a practical 'how to' guide into something more approximating the potential for a personal journey for the individual using the book. This probably was in some respects mirroring my own stage of a developing interest in how this topic both informs and is informed by other areas such as self-esteem and spirituality (Chapter 6) and the links between these personal skills and our political culture (Chapter 1 and Chapter 6).

In writing this book I hoped to cover my own views, and some of the perspectives of writers I most admire on the two areas of the *personal* and the *societal*. While many of the chapters are 'technical', to enable each reader to learn the skills in their own time without the need of a coach or a course, it is my fervent wish that this book goes beyond procedural competence in communication towards an enhanced understanding of some of these more 'macro' and cultural issues. I have attempted to show some connections between the individual and the structures of the society in which we live and work, and I have paid attention both to how each of us can change our personal habits and empower 'self', and in doing so how we can, and do, change the systems of the culture we live in.

Throughout the book I link habits of *power-over* communication with conservative, traditional and patriarchal societies. I advocate a move away from this to a *power-with* way of relating to others, and in Chapter 6, discuss how this may only be possible if we can find our *power-within*—our sense of immanence and self-esteem.

In this book I present to you what I see as fairly compelling reasons to re-seek in yourself connections between self and other, self and self, humankind and universe, the personal and political.

ORGANISATION OF THE BOOK

Chapter 1 (Perspectives on Interpersonal Communication) and Chapter 6 (Self-esteem) are the chapters I would describe as being written at the 'woods' level. Both these chapters look at what has influenced our interpersonal skills from a variety of perspectives—the more usual psychological approach, the sociological view (particularly the critical and feminist perspectives), and from models of organisational reform.

These chapters (in particular, Chapter 6) also introduce the reader to an emerging viewpoint I have termed 'the spiritual'. In this perspective I explore some of the views of the neo-pagan universal spiritualists, and emphasise the possibilities resulting from exploring the connections between our sense of personal power and our ability to relate to people in a way that shares power.

This material is meta-contemporary in human resource development and sacred psychology.

The first and last chapters also pose questions for each of us in terms of where changed interpersonal habits can lead. Notions of reforming an unjust work-place and/or an oppressive society, are described for the reader's information and interest. Some of my own views and the works of other authors in this field are presented quite deliberately to provoke and disturb the reader's thinking beyond their usual comfort zone. In my view, complacency is often one of the biggest demotivators of our desire and capacity for change within our relation-ships and in relation to our culture. Presenting oppositional knowledge to readers can often be 'just the trick' to raise awareness about issues that the person had simply not considered before due to their current life circumstances being 'comfortable'.

Notwithstanding my mission of raising the reader's consciousness, I have also wanted to deliver some prac-tical, down-to-earth and immediately useable skills for home as well as work situations. For example, Chapter 2 (Speaking and Listening Effectively—Assertion . . .) teaches the skills of speaking assertively, ranging from simply learning to declare your own opinions in a way that stands up for your rights (without violating or ignoring the views of others) through to more difficult techniques for confronting people whose behaviour you find unacceptable or whose behaviour needs to be adjusted due to certain performance criteria in the work-place. This chapter gives the practical 'how to's of *power-with* communication.

Chapter 3 deals with the other side of assertion—

listening and responding in a shared power way. Each of the basic skills required for doing this are covered in detail with relevant examples and exercises for the reader's use. My aim was to ensure that the reader could learn the material without me or another teacher being present. Personal empowerment is, in my view, all about having increased choices and skills as opposed to becoming dependent on external resources for your achievements.

Chapter 4 (Advanced Interpersonal Skills) applies the basic skills to advanced situations such as consulting, negotiating, leading and influencing. In this chapter, the speaking skills and listening skills are combined strategically to enable the practitioner to handle resistance and 'difficult' personalities.

Chapter 5 (Leadership and Teamwork) applies the advanced interpersonal skills to the areas of teamwork and leadership. While there are many books available on both these topics, I am aware that some readers need to immediately make the connections between the new skills of assertion and how they apply to their daily management or relationship roles of handling a team of people. This chapter deals with the most common applications of interpersonal skills to problem solving, planning, developing leadership range and handling group dynamics.

For each of the technical chapters (Chapters 2 to 5), the information is constantly linked to issues of *power*. Each chapter gives examples of the traditional style of *power-over* (win–lose dynamics) and suggests alternative ways of relating to people involving *power-with* (win–win, collaborative problem solving).

Chapter 6 deals with self-esteem. In this section of the book a link is drawn between our sense of powerlessness and our win–lose habits in relationships. Many skills and techniques are offered for the reader's choice in redressing low self-esteem. The practicalities offered come from three perspectives—the psychological, the social reform and the spiritual arenas. This chapter touches on some of the history of how our modern Western societies have evolved, and gives some detail of the spiritual connections being sought by many people in need of discovering the connections between their emotional and spiritual lives, and the links between humankind and the planet, indeed the universe.

HOW TO USE THE BOOK

For those of you who seek purely technical details on the *'how to's of speaking and listening assertively*, Chapters 2, 3, 4 and 5 may serve your needs. I personally believe that procedural material ought to be set within context, and that there is value in knowing something of the perspectives that inform the practices—Chapter 1 is such a context. For those of you interested in considering issues of *use and abuse of power* in relationships, the entire book is about both the principles and practices of power.

For readers interested in considering *feminism*, or what feminism offers to communication, Chapters 1 and 6 are useful reading. Those people who are attracted to reading something a 'little different' on the very popular topic of *self-esteem* would also find Chapters 1 and 6 relevant.

1
Perspectives on Interpersonal Communication

YOU MAY HAVE picked up this book because you would like to improve your communication skills at work or because you believe it's possible to improve your relationship with your partner or family. You may be a manager seeking to improve communication in your organisation or a worker who seeks to improve your job prospects and satisfaction through better communication in the workplace.

You may be someone who believes that it is possible for us to change the way we live our lives and even improve the 'health' of society through changing the way we relate to each other. This book speaks to you all and offers improved *interpersonal communication skills* that can and will affect your relationships with people at home and at work and even alter the fabric of our culture. We can change the way we live. One of the secrets is changing the way we speak and listen with others.

This chapter provides a background to interpersonal

communication skills. It is important to realise how the ways we speak have been influenced and it is also interesting to consider how, by simply changing the way we communicate, we can impact on our relationships and perhaps even our entire society.

This chapter poses some critical questions about our society, the personal growth 'industry', and perhaps more importantly, it asks you to question your own values and our cultural 'norms'. For these reasons some readers may find this chapter harder to read than the more 'technical' chapters. That is because what you're reading says some different things from what you have been conditioned to view as usual.

It may not be easy to raise your awareness and grapple with these questions but doing so may uncover a story which needs to be told. Many of us are becoming more and more committed to asking these kinds of questions, sensing they may be at the very heart of what troubles us as a civilisation.

Interpersonal communication is about *power*. Underlying our habits of speech are patterns of use and abuse of power. This book explores ways to achieve sharing of power in relationships. I call this *power-with* communication.

THIS BOOK'S FOCUS

Why do we communicate the way we do? There are different ways of understanding our communication patterns. This book uses three perspectives from the disciplines of *psychology*, *sociology* and *organisational change*. Each of these offers a different way of seeing ourselves, our society and our communication patterns.

- *Psychology*—focusing on humanistic views of how to be and become one's own potential.
- *Sociology*—especially the 'critical' and feminist views of how to change ourselves by challenging and freeing ourselves from oppressive stereotypes and roles.
- *Organisational change*—in particular, workplace reform and the changing nature of the workplace culture in Australian society.

A PSYCHOLOGICAL PERSPECTIVE—THE HUMAN POTENTIAL MOVEMENT

The main aim of this book is to give you increased awareness of the choices available to you for enhanced interpersonal ability in your relationships. You and I as individuals, have *choices* and *skills* and therefore have the opportunity to change our current repertoire of habits and patterns. In other words, we are able to grow and develop by learning new techniques for communicating with the people in our lives.

This is the perspective of what is often called the 'Human Potential Movement', which maintains that each of us is ultimately *responsible* for our own lives, and that we need to exercise free will to be and become our own potential.

In counselling, many therapists will coach the client to challenge and change habits that are not working in either their home or work life. Similarly, in personal growth or professional development courses, the trainer is likely to encourage clients to find their needs and wants, and then set goals using inner and external resources to achieve them.

A significant part of such courses is usually devoted

Figure 1.1   The psychology of personal responsibility

to issues of communicating more effectively. It is common for many training programs to ask people to clarify their needs and dreams, *then* to communicate them openly and honestly *and then* to be prepared to take action to get their needs met.

There are numerous books, tapes, videos and courses available in this area of 'popular' psychology and its application to motivational training and business development. Most of these advocate developing our *power-within* via use of new skills and 'personal growth' techniques. This is because the essence of psychology is that 'solutions' lie in *personal change*.

Figure 1.1 shows the 'self' in apparent isolation. To change the 'self' requires using new choices and skills. However, later in this chapter (see Figs 1.3 and 1.4) the impact of the social context is made apparent.

Figure 1.2 Developing my potential

NEEDS	RESOURCES	

• Dreams
• Wishes
• Biological
• Self-awareness INNER
• To be and
  become our
  potential
	• To change
	• To grow
	• To learn
	• Self-direction SELF
	• Motivation
	• Drive to self-
	  actualise
		Health/
		Happiness
		
		OR
		
		Effectiveness/
		Productivity

• Social
• Positive regard
  from others
• Roles/definitions OUTER
• Material possessions
• Employability
• Meaningful career
	• Others
	• Environment
	• Work
	• Home OTHER
	• Commitments
	• Professional
	  development	

Personal growth

A fairly simple psychological model, Figure 1.2 represents the marriage of *needs* with *resources* to lead towards increased *health* or *effectiveness*.

When reading this model, you will notice that needs are divided up into 'inner' and 'outer'. It is common in the human potential movement to consider both *inner* needs—those coming from within the *self*—and *outer* needs—those involving the desire to comply with social norms and rituals to gain acceptance. Resources are also divided into 'self' and 'other'. *Self* is the ability and potential that lie within you which can be utilised in relative isolation. *Other* is the ability to utilise people and materials outside the self to assist in achieving your needs.

In the area of professional development, psychology models have been used as the basis of training under the 'Human Resource Development' banner. Courses centre around people learning improved communication skills to deal more effectively with clients, staff and colleagues. Participants are taught goal setting, action planning and time management, but there is particular emphasis on *interpersonal communication* so that people can become better listeners, overcome conflict and solve problems as part of a team.

In a nutshell, the psychological perspective on inter-personal communication skills suggests the ability to communicate assertively is a resource that the 'self' can use to become empowered to improve relationships and to deal with conflict both personally and professionally.

Assertion is defined as a 'win–win' style of co-oper-ation. Throughout this book I also use the term 'power-with' to describe the philosophy and practice of sharing power with others.

A SOCIOLOGICAL PERSPECTIVE— AN UNJUST SOCIETY

Many sociologists would view the psychological perspec-tive as limited, or naive, because it appears to view the individual as existing in a vacuum, ignorant of environ-mental shaping. Sociologists often see the 'human potential movement' as placing too much emphasis on the *individual's* need to change in what they view as a hostile and unfair world. Some say the self-help focus knowingly or unwittingly places a burden on the indi-vidual because it assumes the fault or blame lies with

Figure 1.3 Choice within boundaries

each person. This can result in protection of the status quo of a socially unjust society.

A sociological perspective places the individual within the context of an environment which moulds and shapes the individual, causing feelings of powerlessness and low self-esteem. For example, consider how many people in your workplace have more power than you and consequently affect your choices and skills. Systems, structures, regulations, clients, bosses—all have this kind of impact on a daily basis. When you leave work and go home you are being shaped and affected by societal norms and values, rituals, stereotypes and roles.

Figure 1.3 shows where the individual is placed within societal or institutional surrounds. The arrows indicate the environmental arena acting on the personal arena. This idea—that we have choices within social limitations and boundaries—can fit well with the psychological perspective of developing your potential. In essence, the inner circle is the psychology of the *personal* and the outer circle is the politics of the *institutional* and *societal*.

Figure 1.4 represents the dilemma between the personal and political as a *tension*. In other words, there is an ongoing tussle between the will of self and the will of the culture in which the individual is operating.

A sociological stance involves a deep questioning of the prevailing norms of 'society' and the lies and misrepresentations that support them. It encourages us to ask who is winning and who is losing in the system, and what responsibilities we have to make it different. The same interpersonal skills we wish to have for personal empowerment can be used to provoke and disturb cultural norms and to challenge win–lose dynamics. We can raise awareness for ourselves and others of the external forces which damage our self-esteem and limit our choices.

The essence of sociology is that solutions lie in *societal* and *political change*.

The way to develop *power-within* ourselves is considered to involve becoming 'conscious' of the brainwashing we are subjected to, taking back our power by making enlightened choices and demanding reform to the 'system'.

Figure 1.4   The tension between the individual and the institution

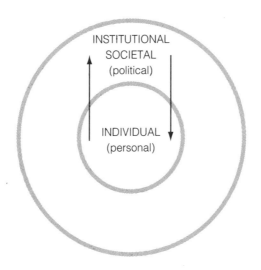

Social justice

Currently, a lot is being said and written on the topic of social justice in most public and private sector work institutions. The main reason for this is the number of legislative reforms impacting on the Australian work-force relating to issues of social justice, equity and equal employment opportunity. Employers are being told they need to comply with certain laws and regulations redressing perceived social 'wrongs'. Australian culture is starting to become aware of the unfair nature of society and the inequity of many of its norms, rituals and values.

In our country, certain people are recognised as more 'correct', 'usual' or 'normal'. These people or groups are upheld as the cultural norm against which other people are compared. Comparison most commonly results in the 'other' groups being labelled as less desirable, incorrect, or somehow second class. The words *dominant* vs *marginal* groups have been coined as a way of explaining this phenomena.

If we consider questions of sex, age, race, sexual preference and so on, Figure 1.5 represents a fairly common understanding of those in our society who seem to be more advantaged and those regarded as 'losers'. Figure 1.5 shows us living in a sexist, racist, ethnocentric, ageist, classist, heterosexist, scientist etc. etc. culture. The people with most of the disadvantages tend to be any of us who do not fit in all the dominant group categories.

Some people who study these issues point out that there may be 'no one more oppressed than the oppressor'. This means that even if you are in many of the dominant categories, you are also likely to suffer low self-esteem for fear of losing your power base. In other words, if you believe in the more dominant groups' opinions as absolute truths, you are likely to be constantly striving to achieve them. Therefore you can never feel okay about yourself because absolute truths are not real. They are socially contrived illusions.

What Figure 1.5 indicates is the real unfairness of the 'system'. For example, approximately 51 per cent of

**Figure 1.5   Dominant and marginal groups in
Australian society**

DOMINANT GROUPS	'MARGINAL' GROUPS
• White	• Non-white
• Anglo-Saxon/Celt	• Other ethnic backgrounds
• Male	• Female
• Middle aged	• Younger or older
• Middle class	• Working class
• Heterosexual	• Lesbian or gay male
• With a degree	• Non-tertiary educated
• 'Healthy'	• Differently abled
• Etc.	• Etc.

society is not male. Australia has a truly multicultural
mix of inhabitants of whom only a small percentage is
middle class. By far, the majority is working class. It is
commonly accepted that approximately one in eight
people are not heterosexual, but have a same-sex preference. When we consider these kinds of figures, it
becomes clear that what we take as 'just the way things
are', or the 'natural order of things', is an ideological
distortion which does not evenly serve the needs of all
people. This practice of unequal power relations where
some people win and other people lose is called
'hegemony'. It is aided by our educational systems and
multimedia sources, and is played out in our workplace
and our families, which are bastions of ongoing hegemony.

Increasing numbers of Australians, either because of
legislative reform and/or their awareness being raised on
these issues, are acting at either a *personal* or an *institutional* level to make changes to this system of unfairness.

The 'cause' of poor communication

Increasing numbers of people want to learn changed/ improved/assertive interpersonal communication skills, for their personal and business use. Over the past ten years I have heard thousands of people talk of their need for improved communication in their relationships, their career, and in particular, in dealing with what they call 'difficult' personalities.

Most people assume the cause of their communication issues lies in poor habits, not being in touch enough with what they want, or as a result of low self-esteem. This is consistent with the *psychological* perspective. A *sociological* view of 'cause' sees our communication habits as part of the flawed and distorted way our culture teaches us to relate to people, so that some benefit at the expense of most others. In other words, you and I are not taught to be assertive by our role models because the existing system prefers we remain disempowered. While we busy ourselves with 'tact', 'niceness' or alternatively 'being correct' or 'winning' (various forms of win–lose), we are distanced from the possibilities of co-operative and collaborative connections with others—win–win or *power-with* others.

My view involves a combination of both perspectives. I believe ineffective communication habits are part of our cultural learning and that most of us have picked up communication habits that are about winning or losing, in relation to another party. This distortion in the way that we relate to each other underpins patriarchal power systems and serves the interests of 'power brokers' within our work institutions and society as a whole.

12

However, we do not need to continue with such patterns.

I believe in changing our way of communicating from win–lose or lose–win into what I call 'power-with' or *collaborative problem solving*. Indeed, I view changed interpersonal habits as a truly empowering opportunity for the individual, and perhaps eventually for the society (see Figure 1.7 on page 18). For over ten years, I have personally witnessed people changing their relationships and personal self-esteem by changing the way they communicate.

I see these changed interpersonal habits of assertive speaking and listening (found in Chapters 2 to 5), as enabling each of us to relate better to ourselves and voice our opinions to others, without 'beating' them or allowing our stance to be 'beaten'.

Additionally, speaking assertively disturbs the cultural habits of unequal power relations and breaks down the traditional regimes of dominant groups advantaged over the less powerful. Over time, a critical mass of people is built up which is not prepared to tolerate the status quo and, as individuals, are therefore contributing to change at a macro and societal level.

What feminism offers communication

The word feminism conjures up different things for different people. In reality there is not a single group of 'feminists' who believe in the same things. There are of course many tenets of feminism with various beliefs and practices associated with them. For example, a 'liberal' feminist will have some very different viewpoints and will exhibit different behaviours from a 'Marxist' or a 'poststructural' feminist.

Feminism, like all philosophies, has some very valuable things to offer us if we can afford to listen. One of the problems with reacting negatively to a term such as 'feminism' is that we miss opportunities to learn from another perspective. It has been suggested that the word is deliberately 'given a bad name' by those who have the most to lose by acceptance of its philosophy.

In fact, feminism is embraced by many men, especially businessmen who are increasingly comfortable with its theory. Some have embraced many of its practices as helpful ways to solve problems collaboratively at work and in personal relationships. Feminist principles and practices are increasingly common, and even mainstream, in areas such as business ethics, organisational development, human resource development, and environmentalism.

A simple, yet fairly universal, definition of feminism sees it as preferring non-violent (or non-aggressive) means and solutions for problem solving. Most feminists are against *patriarchy*, the culture of beliefs and behaviours which values win–lose solutions. A feminist perspective positions non-assertive communication (passive or aggressive) as part of the patriarchal system where 'masculine category' values and traits are upheld as best (see Figure 1.6 on page 15). Some strands of feminism fit the notion that our interpersonal skills act as a tool of patriarchal unfairness; that is, the way we speak tells a story about the nature of society, work institutions and common relationship habits.

Incidentally, you may notice patriarchy is defined

Figure 1.6 A comparison between patriarchy and feminism

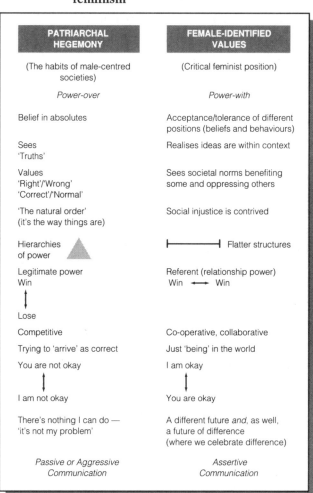

PATRIARCHAL HEGEMONY	FEMALE-IDENTIFIED VALUES
(The habits of male-centred societies)	(Critical feminist position)
Power-over	*Power-with*
Belief in absolutes	Acceptance/tolerance of different positions (beliefs and behaviours)
Sees 'Truths'	Realises ideas are within context
Values 'Right'/'Wrong' 'Correct'/'Normal'	Sees societal norms benefiting some and oppressing others
'The natural order' (it's the way things are)	Social injustice is contrived
Hierarchies of power	⊢———⊣ Flatter structures
Legitimate power Win	Referent (relationship power) Win ⟷ Win
Lose	
Competitive	Co-operative, collaborative
Trying to 'arrive' as correct	Just 'being' in the world
You are not okay	I am okay
I am not okay	You are okay
There's nothing I can do — 'it's not my problem'	A different future *and*, as well, a future of difference (where we celebrate difference)
Passive or Aggressive Communication	*Assertive Communication*

15

here in its broader sense—not just about male values. It is overly simplistic and inaccurate for feminism to be seen as 'anti-men'. It's not about men or individual males at all. Many females are patriarchs. Many men abhor our patriarchal culture and work hard at a personal or political level for change to the system of patriarchy.

Patriarchal hegemony is defined as the masculine category or male-centredness that creates unequal and unjust power relationships between people and groups in society. Figure 1.6 shows the habits of patriarchal societies on the left-hand side and details the possibilities of more 'feminine categories' and behaviours as an alternative. You will notice that this figure is a dichotomy—presented as either/or—and is set up as opposites. This is a strictly limited way to view our lives, and the postmodern and poststructural feminists strongly urge us to stop seeing things in relation to another, or as a category in opposition to another. Instead, they urge us to view things simply as 'is'. Nonetheless, Figure 1.6 is offered as a basic understanding of patriarchy vs female-centred values and views.

You will notice that patriarchy is about 'black and white' thinking, dividing up into parts, reducing down into compartments, and a search for 'god's eye' rational 'truths'. It upholds thinking as superior to emotion. It values knowledge as objective scientific fact as opposed to subjective experience. Under this system we see *language* as being of secondary importance, believing that thought precedes language and that language is 'innocent'.

Consider how innocent it really is to keep using the

word 'he' while saying that it is *not* discriminatory and is *meant* to denote both he and she. This way it has been easy for women to be written out of history, while being told that no harm is meant by this. How many people of both sexes commonly state that they mean 'nothing' by using words such as 'young lady', 'honey', and 'mankind'? Women are labelled 'overly sensitive' or 'man haters' if they point out the inappropriateness and discriminatory nature of these terms. Similarly, if a nurse is described as 'a little nurse', a factory foreman as 'the gay guy' or a child as 'her half-caste cousin' discriminatory language is being used. Doing so perpetuates an unfair social order.

The female-identified values and behaviours in Figure 1.6 denote a more holistic and integrated awareness of political and social context. This alternative says that there is no real truth, and knowledge is not innocent but is ideological, benefiting some at the expense of others. This system attempts to integrate body, emotion and cognitive functioning. There is desire to deconstruct, disrupt, and keep things in flux to constantly critique what is going on. Language is seen as preceding thought. The way we speak is a very powerful perpetuator of our culture at home and at work and has major effects on the way we think and behave.

Notice that passive and aggressive (non-assertive) communication are linked to patriarchal societal norms. Assertive communication—upholding one's rights whilst respecting the rights of other people—is situated as a more female-identified value and behaviour.

Figure 1.7 gives some details of actual communication habits and patterns that belong to these three

Figure 1.7 Styles of communication and power

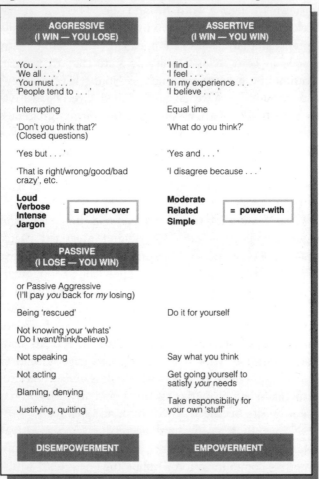

AGGRESSIVE (I WIN — YOU LOSE)	ASSERTIVE (I WIN — YOU WIN)
'You . . .' 'We all . . .' 'You must . . .' 'People tend to . . .'	'I find . . .' 'I feel . . .' 'In my experience . . .' 'I believe . . .'
Interrupting	Equal time
'Don't you think that?' (Closed questions)	'What do you think?'
'Yes but . . .'	'Yes and . . .'
'That is right/wrong/good/bad crazy', etc.	'I disagree because . . .'
Loud Verbose Intense Jargon = power-over	**Moderate Related Simple** = power-with

PASSIVE (I LOSE — YOU WIN)	
or Passive Aggressive (I'll pay *you* back for *my* losing)	
Being 'rescued'	Do it for yourself
Not knowing your 'whats' (Do I want/think/believe)	
Not speaking	Say what you think
Not acting	Get going yourself to satisfy *your* needs
Blaming, denying	Take responsibility for your own 'stuff'
Justifying, quitting	

DISEMPOWERMENT	EMPOWERMENT

18

'categories' (passive, aggressive and assertive communication). Chapter 3 will help you to make sense of these styles of speaking and listening.

In summary, most feminist positions suggest that unequal power relations are maintained by a lack of criticism of society's norms, understandings, and values. The promotion of this culture by media and educational systems result in a deep saturation of our consciousness. We end up with an unquestioning acceptance that the way things are is 'natural' rather than being seen as a distortion that does not serve the interests of all equitably. So called 'commonsense', especially in terms of beliefs, values, relationships, and *language*, is seen as the way patriarchal societies are sustained.

Assertion is a significant communication tool to serve both the individual and the society in changing to become more just for all.

A *political vision*

Many economically developed Western countries have been undergoing considerable philosophical changes. Past values were based on accepting the 'establishment' where there were absolute moral principles, competitive individualism, desire for stability, abuse of the environment and a strong focus on economic security. These so-called absolutes in some areas are being replaced with preference for consensus, desire for social reform, emphasis on personal development, quality of life, interdependence and appreciation of the earth and our connections to nature cycles.

In both the social and organisational arenas, people in Western cultures are moving from traditional values and practices towards 'new age' habits of *choice* and *responsibility*. Words such as 'choice' and acceptance of 'consequences' for such choices are becoming commonplace in our relationships, family life and work interactions. At the same time there is a swing away from following the teachings, laws, and regulations laid down by power brokers such as the boss, the headmaster, the father, the church. This represents a significant move towards people learning to wrestle with their own conscience in terms of decision making. These changes serve as attempts to move away from a *power-over* culture towards a community that values both *power-within* the individual and *power-with* others.

The interpersonal skills of assertion are consistent with this culture shift. Collective ways of solving problems and making decisions that are based in sharing and connection are being sought in many areas of our society.

Who's winning, who's losing—deconstruction

Increasing numbers of people are having their 'comfort zones' challenged by those of us who are interested in disturbing society's power to mould and shape people. Many of us are learning to ask ourselves questions of what we believe, why we believe what we do, and who will be advantaged and disadvantaged by our values and actions.

The process of critical thinking is known as *deconstruction*. One of its aims is to offset the tendency to think in categories, which often end up being about right and wrong, good and bad, correct and incorrect. Maintaining this state of flux or deconstruction is an antidote to legitimate power. The power brokers in our

Figure 1.8 Steps for deconstruction (critical thinking)

1 Identify all possible positions in the topic.
2 Where do you stand? And where else?
3 Where do your ideas come from?
   (Where historically have your ideas come from?)
4 Whose interests are served/not served by these
   positions? (Who's winning and who's losing?)
5 *Goal setting* — What do I now believe and why?
   Therefore what action will I take/not take?

culture are being challenged and some are challenging themselves about their position. Figure 1.8 represents the steps for deconstruction that are used by many of the more aware teachers, political activists and academics. We are beginning to see some senior and middle managers committed to this type of process to enable changes to their company culture towards a more egalitarian one.

ORGANISATIONAL CHANGE

Workplace reform

As part of this shift in the values of Western nations we are seeing most of our public and private sector work organisations undergoing change. Some companies and departments have been attending to strategic planning, assessment of values, missions, goals and objectives. Others have been focused mainly on their systems and structures. The word 'restructure' has become an almost daily utterance in many public service departments.

Many public departments are undergoing social justice and equal opportunity policy development to conform with anti-discrimination laws. Other organisations, particularly in the private sector, are interested in missions that involve peace, harmony, ecological survival and overturning oppressive power relationships both with their clients and in the workplace.

Increasingly, we are seeing organisations attending to a newer focus called 'culture change'. This involves changing the beliefs and behaviours of the personnel in an institution and encompasses new expertise in interpersonal communication skills and managerial competence.

Quite apart from the need for compliance with industrial legislation, corporate life is attempting to more closely mimic the changed nature of its client base. Our social culture has changed to the extent that people are much more aware of their rights and needs. They want to be listened to by service providers and are asserting a requirement for improved 'customer service'. Management focus has shifted its attention to the client's needs.

Culture change

Significant changes to culture have become apparent in management development. Managers are being asked to become much better at interpersonal and team communications and less reliant on their legitimate power base in rank, qualifications and experience.

Figure 1.9 represents the kind of shift occurring in most industries.

You will notice the shift is a move away from man-

Figure 1.9   Culture change in management

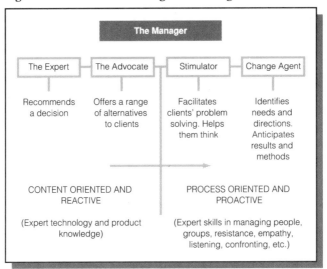

agers simply *telling* people what to do towards a more collaborative process. It is not just managers who are being asked to change and broaden their thinking and actions, however, most staff are being expected to develop the full range illustrated in Figure 1.9.

In many industries there is a shift from a management to a leadership style. Figure 1.10 represents the type of culture change being asked of many managers and staff. Notice there is a swing away from the more black and white, absolutist and *power-over* ways of thinking and acting. The trend is towards a problem-solving, developmental and *power-with* approach. You will note that aggressive and passive (win–lose) ways of communicating are positioned in the left-hand column as part of the more traditional style of management.

Figure 1.10 Changing culture

THE MANAGER	THE LEADER
Tells	Coaches
Sells	Facilitates
The boss	Empowers
Plans	Develops
Organises	Consults
Controls	Process observer
Diagnoses	Notices
Labels	Observes
Interprets	Is aware of
Trees	Woods
Parent/Child	Adult
Blames	Take
Denies	responsibility
Justifies	for your
Quits	actions
COMPETITIVE	COLLABORATIVE CO-OPERATIVE

	Role and Systems		Missions and Service	
	Power		People	

AGGRESSIVE AND PASSIVE 'Power-over'	ASSERTIVE 'Power-with'

In some places, hierarchies of power are being broken down. We are seeing 'flatter structures' and responsibility for choices and decisions being made more at the local level. Companies are experiencing a change of focus which is beyond doing what the boss tells you (*power*) and sticking to your duty description (*role*) and emphasises attending to the real needs of clients by making decisions that are constantly related back to the core values and mission. Still other more enlightened organisations are focusing on the needs of their people by trialing ways of increasing staff's happiness and personal empowerment. Some are allowing staff to choose their own hours, pay, work environment and tasks to be performed.

There is also a phenomenon called 'backlash' that occurs in response to changes such as these. Backlash is where people react in ways that are attempts to push us back to the old 'safe' ways again—ways that can continue to benefit only some at the expense of many. One of the most common forms of backlash is by discrediting new ideas and 'different' people. There are many ways of slowing down change towards these more contemporary values, including most forms of active or passive resistance.

Figure 1.11 represents this trend in company culture change as represented by a well-known organisational consultant, Roger Harrison. Notice that the move is away from 'power' and 'role' (the more traditional style of culture) towards 'mission' and 'support'.

If we can achieve this type of cultural combination, work would be a place that is not only concerned with achieving what the clients need, it would also support the people who work there, making it a place of enjoyment where we can develop personally and professionally. This type of culture would treat each person with respect, build in choices and allow each

Figure 1.11 Roger Harrison's model—organisational culture

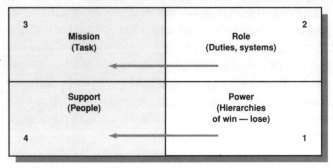

person to have genuine responsibility and support from other workers.

To achieve this, we would require changed *interpersonal communication skills* consistent with this type of culture. Assertion skills are about collaborative, co-operative problem solving. They encourage win–win and the sharing of power as opposed to one person winning and the other losing. The skills detailed in the remainder of this book are essential tools for more 'modern' leadership and organisational culture change as well as an empowering opportunity for each of us.

A change in interpersonal communication habits may be uncomfortable for some people who have been used to win–lose dynamics. Assertive speech may at first threaten and disturb the existing system of power brokers. Some employees report they receive some initial negative feedback when they apply some of their newly learned interpersonal skills but that this passes fairly quickly because the skills work well for *both* parties. Almost without exception, people prefer to continue with assertion skills because they find they achieve better results in their relationships regardless of the initial discomfort experienced by some of their bosses or friends.

In my opinion as a management consultant, the last ten years have seen our workplace culture become genuinely more in need of and appreciative of assertive communicators. The following chapters will explain what constitutes *'power-with' communication* and give details of the practicalities of speaking and listening in this way.

AN EMERGING PERSPECTIVE

There is another perspective that both informs and is potentially informed by the notions of use/abuse of power. It is variously called 'new age', 'universal spirituality', 'sacred psychology', 'women's spirituality' and 'pagan'. This spiritual perspective provides some of the history behind the way we communicate today as well as offering some exciting new possibilities of our potential to relate to each other in ways that truly share power.

In Chapter 6, I discuss in some detail how early 'primitive' civilisations were characterised by some very different ways of experiencing and using power. People saw themselves as having power 'inside' them that was connected to the power and mystery of the cosmos. They saw themselves as part of a life/death/rebirth cycle where rather than controlling the environment they felt they were part of it and responsible to it.

There were times when 'power' was viewed as available *within* the person as opposed to our patriarchal ways of seeing power as found *outside* in the structures, systems and institutions of our society. It is possible that the 'earth religions' of earlier civilisations have some offerings for how we can communicate in ways that reconnect parts of ourselves (emotional, social, mental, physical and spiritual) and allow for each of us to connect with other people, the planet and all its creatures.

In the final chapter of this book I devote emphasis to exploring the link between high self-esteem (feeling *power-within*) and the ability to communicate with others in a sharing of power (*power-with*) style. I detail how our habits of communicating in win–lose ways may be due to the sense of powerlessness that comes as a consequence of the type of culture we live in.

These so-called 'new age' perspectives are just beginning to be heard in mainstream management training and human resource development. Some areas of industry, particularly leadership, are beginning to grapple with putting back connections that our culture may have been splitting apart for many centuries.

I am personally attracted to encompassing this more spiritual perspective with the other views from psychology, sociology and organisational change. I sense that each of the perspectives are part of a greater 'whole' and that to continue to see each as separate is limited and unhelpful in creating change. The spiritual perspective is broad enough to accommodate the views of those who see our communication habits as about 'poor' personal choice, those who see it as a consequence of 'poor' conditioning from an unfair social order, and those who see our interpersonal skills as a symptom of our spiritual withering.

2
Speaking and Listening Effectively— Assertion . . .

THE DIFFERENCE BETWEEN ASSERTIVE AND NON-ASSERTIVE COMMUNICATION

Assertion is one of the most misunderstood concepts and sets of skills in the communication arena. You are about to learn what assertion *really* is about as opposed to the myths and deliberate misconceptions that surround this very worthwhile and practical tool. (You may find it interesting to consider the questions of who is winning and who is losing by such misunderstandings, and why there is a lack of teaching of this skill in our schools and other institutions. Which people in our society have the most to lose by you and I becoming more effective in our relationships with them?)

The two sides of assertion

Figure 2.1 shows that assertion involves both talking and listening components.

The talking side of assertion involves owning your own statements—so-called 'I statements'. In a variety of circumstances and situations, assertion will ensure that you can be effective in every situation. The *talking skills* will be covered in this chapter, starting from the easy skills of simply stating your position on any given topic through to the more difficult techniques of confronting someone whose behaviour is unacceptable to you or who is violating one of your needs or 'rights.

The other side of communication involves *listening and responding*. Each of these techniques is a crucial skill in its own right which can be used to great effect when combined in the order followed in this chapter. This will give you a helpful process design for counselling a

Figure 2.1: The two sides of assertion

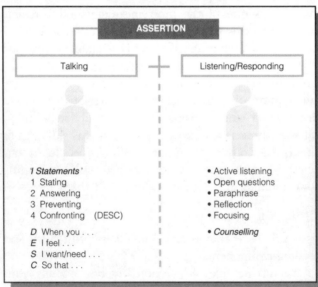

person with a problem in either their home or work lives.

Assertion is an antidote to our cultural habits of win–lose, *power-over* styles of relating. Assertion is about power sharing with others.

Talking and listening skills later will be combined in a certain formula to comprise the advanced interpersonal skills of *pacing and leading* and dealing with *resistance* (see Chapter 6). So, while these skills are tools of empowerment, they also are necessary prerequisites for the advanced interpersonal skills of leading, negotiating, handling conflict, teaching and influence.

My style

Although I am speaking to you as such as you read this book, I'm doing it in the form of a written discourse. I have grappled with the question of how to write this chapter and wondered how I might model the behaviours I am advocating. For example, will I write 'I believe that "I statements" are more effective because I have found . . .' I have decided to use the third person for the more technical chapters (3, 4 and 5); that is, 'I statements are a more open and direct way of indicating your position . . .'

In speech the use of this style often sounds absolutist—as though you are speaking from the lofty heights of 'the truth' of the matter (aggressive not assertive). For the purpose of this book, however, which is in written form, it will be more straightforward if I advocate a position on these techniques and allow you to try out the 'how to's and the 'formulas', notice the consequences you're getting and in turn make up your mind whether the results are worth you changing your old habits more permanently to take on board these assertive skills.

Do try the skills before deciding they won't work. I have heard some people say they won't bother having a go at speaking or listening differently because they think it might be too hard to maintain or they worry it might sound different to their friends or their staff. Actually *doing* the skill is the best way (perhaps even the only way) of finding out what really happens rather than what you imagine.

SOME DEFINITIONS

Aggressive patterns

If you are aggressive or have a habit of falling into aggressive patterns of communication at times, you will stand up for your rights while ignoring or even violating the rights of other people.

By rights I mean your needs, wants, values or opinions. You are entitled to your own views, which is why I call them your rights.

As Figure 2.2 indicates, aggressive people are not necessarily loud or hostile in appearance. Aggression occurs any time that you win and the other person, as a consequence of your actions, is set up as the loser. A simple example of aggression would be if your talking takes up most of the air space and doesn't allow the other party to communicate equally with you. That is not to say there are some people who do not wish to speak half or even nearly half of the time, but aggression is about using techniques that maintain your air space

Figure 2.2: Aggressive communication

AGGRESSIVE: I stand up for my rights while violating or ignoring your rights.

Most aggressive people do *not* appear hostile or even loud. Aggression occurs any time you put down, or violate, another's needs.

For example:

Interrupting — really says that what I have to say is more important than what you have to say.

Speaking for others — assumes that others will or should share my opinion (e.g. 'This is the kind of thing that gets you really upset').

Being dogmatic or absolute assumes that there is only one 'right' opinion about a subject — mine!
(e.g. 'You can't have flexitime because people take advantage of it').

MY RIGHTS   YOUR RIGHTS

and deny the other person's. For example, some people speak quickly or without appearing to pause for breath. The consequence of this can be that the other person feels that they do not have an opportunity to be heard and cannot enter the conversation or survive the inter-action.

Another typical form of aggression is interrupting people before they have finished what they were going to say. If you indulge in this pattern you are sending a message to anybody involved that you think what you have to say is more important than the other person's point of view, and are demonstrating this by beginning your discourse prior to their finishing. Ending sentences for other people or speaking louder than the other

33

person's voice is another habit of denying the other person.

Perhaps the most common habit of Australian cultural communication in work and home environments is the pattern people have of not owning their own statements. Instead of saying 'I think . . .' or 'I feel . . .', many people use 'you statements'; for example, 'You know what it's like. You just have to do it, don't you?' or 'Well, we all find that we can't . . .' Later in this chapter I will address in detail how to speak in non-common cultural terms, that is, how to speak truly assertively by owning your own point of view.

To summarise, *aggressive* communication is where *I win–you lose* dynamics are occurring in the interaction and therefore the interaction is *power-over*.

Passive patterns

If you give away or defer your wants, needs, opinions or rights to another party you are acting passively or have a habit of passive communication. Passive people do not necessarily look shy and retiring as indicated in Figure 2.3, but are indulging in an *I lose–you win* dynamic. A common pattern of passivity that exists in our society is where somebody doesn't say what it is that they want or need. Often that person is later angry that their needs weren't realised by the other person in the relationship. If they then 'pay them back' for not guessing what they needed, we have what we call '*passive/aggressive*' communication. This is a combination that is common to many women in our society. For example, women are socialised into being 'nice', which often means not saying what they want, or being uncomfortable to

Figure 2.3: Passive communication

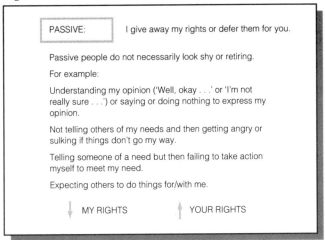

| PASSIVE: | I give away my rights or defer them for you. |

Passive people do not necessarily look shy or retiring.

For example:

Understanding my opinion ('Well, okay . . .' or 'I'm not really sure . . .') or saying or doing nothing to express my opinion.

Not telling others of my needs and then getting angry or sulking if things don't go my way.

Telling someone of a need but then failing to take action myself to meet my need.

Expecting others to do things for/with me.

MY RIGHTS   YOUR RIGHTS

disagree with someone, particularly a man. The consequence to the women is self-anger (conscious or unconscious) and they may take it out on or *payback* the other person.

It is also passive if you know what you want, state it assertively, but then fail to take action to meet your own needs. For example, you want to go for a drive in the mountains on Sunday and say so with 'I statements' which ensure your own needs and wants when you communicate, but you fail to go for the drive because your partner would prefer to go fishing. It becomes passive/aggressive if, in addition to failing to meet your own needs, you then stay home and sulk to pay that person back, or go fishing with them but behave in a 'difficult' manner.

These dynamics all result in win–lose or lose–win

dynamics for both parties. Passive habits, like aggressive ones, is *power-over* communication.

ASSERTION

Assertive patterns—the essence of being effective

Assertive people stand up for their rights while always upholding the rights of the other person.

As Figure 2.4 indicates, assertive communication is about accepting your ideas and your needs as your own and allowing other people to be different if they choose to be. Assertive people believe and/or indicate in their speech patterns that they are interested in win–win solutions or collaborative, co-operative action. This is the style of communication I call *power-with*.

Figure 2.4: Assertive communication

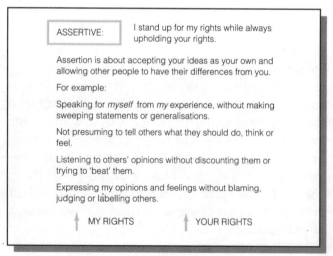

> ASSERTIVE: I stand up for my rights while always upholding your rights.
>
> Assertion is about accepting your ideas as your own and allowing other people to have their differences from you.
>
> For example:
>
> Speaking for *myself* from *my* experience, without making sweeping statements or generalisations.
>
> Not presuming to tell others what they should do, think or feel.
>
> Listening to others' opinions without discounting them or trying to 'beat' them.
>
> Expressing my opinions and feelings without blaming, judging or labelling others.
>
> ↑ MY RIGHTS   ↑ YOUR RIGHTS

Compromise, incidentally, is only one choice when you are an assertive person. It is not necessarily the preferred choice of many people because, remember, even if compromise is shared, the best you are going to receive is 50 per cent of what you want. For many of us this is not acceptable, although in our society we tend to be conditioned into believing compromise is the best solution. It is possible to have all of what you want, and to allow the other person to have all of what they want, through using assertive problem-solving processes and communication techniques.

On the left side of Figure 2.5 the habits of many Australians are shown. Effective assertive communication techniques are shown on the right.

Notice the habits of the left side of the model.

'You know how you feel. You just feel terrible, don't you?' and 'You just don't know what to do about it do you . . .?'

This is not assertive since it assumes your opinion is shared by everyone. Therefore, you are making sweeping generalisations, or speaking from a 'god's eye' (patriarchal) perspective and not respecting the rights of others to choose to be the same or different.

Figure 2.5: Cultural patterns

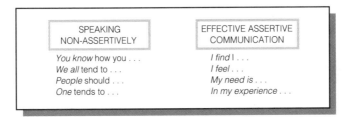

SPEAKING NON-ASSERTIVELY	EFFECTIVE ASSERTIVE COMMUNICATION
You know how you . . .	*I find I . . .*
We all tend to . . .	*I feel . . .*
People should . . .	*My need is . . .*
One tends to . . .	*In my experience . . .*

37

More appropriate is the use of 'I statements'. 'I statements' are the essence of assertion, because they indicate to any listener that you are speaking for *yourself*, from your own experience, without presuming to tell other people what they are like, or how they should think or feel. For example, simply saying:

> 'I find that I don't know what to do in these situations. I end up doing nothing.'

Not only is this more effective communication but it allows the other party to actually get to know you through honest personal disclosure.

The third example of Figure 2.5 is another common habit of non-assertive communication in our culture.

> 'People should realise that what they have to do is . . .'

This is going a step further from generalising your experiences onto the entire human race. It also includes a judgment, or advice (which actually tells more about *you* than it does about the 'absolute truth' of the matter).

The assertive way to communicate with the other person is by saying:

> 'My need is to . . .' or 'I wish I could have more of . . .'

The final example used in Figure 2.5 is a distancing technique to ensure that the other person is kept away from you. Some listeners may hear it as a technique of superiority over another person when:

> 'One tends to feel that one should in certain circumstances concern oneself with . . .'

38

It is far more straightforward and assertive to say:

'In my experience I have found . . .'

Remember, assertion also requires the ability to *listen*. Assertive listening is active listening without trying to discount or beat the other person by listening only enough to gather evidence. Chapter 4 will deal in great detail with the skills that comprise assertive listening.

Assertion is about I win–you win dynamics, and involves expressing opinions and feelings without blaming, judging or labelling, and allowing them the opportunity to have their point of view in the interaction.

Before you speak . . .

Assertion is not simply about how you speak. To be an assertive person you need to be able to first work out what is your point of view, then speak assertively, and finally take action that is consistent with your stated needs (and live with the consequences). Figure 2.6 outlines this process.

Some people believe that you ought to improve your sense of self (your needs, wants, views and self-esteem) *before* you start using assertive 'I statements'. In other words, some people wait until they have got themselves 'in better order' before they consider changing the way that they speak. I do *not agree* with this approach. For a start I think waiting until you get your sense of self improved before you begin to communicate differently can end up being either a very long wait or a good excuse for not actually beginning to change your behaviour.

I don't think it matters whether you start working

Figure 2.6: The steps in being assertive

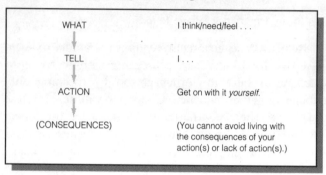

out your 'whats'—which will in turn enable you to speak with assertive 'I statements', or whether you work the other way around—which is to begin to own your own statements and in saying 'I . . .' find your sense of self there and then because of the way that you're constructing your sentence. In fact, many people report they feel much more in touch with who they really are as a consequence of beginning to own their own statements.

Some of us have difficulty with the first step towards being assertive, that is, we don't know what our 'whats' are. Many of us get over-socialised by our conditioning processes in life, and can lose touch with self and what are our needs, wants and ambitions. Many people express difficulty in being sure of their stance on any issue because they have been strongly conditioned into the rituals, norms and stereotypes of their family, employer and society. This is particularly evident in sex-role stereotypes where, for example, many men feel that their 'whats' are really what they *should* be doing to be a 'good man' (for instance, being strong and decisive), and many women feel that their primary 'what' is to be liked and be seen as 'nice' which is manifested by being non-assertive in their communication styles.

Raising your consciousness to challenge and perhaps change some of the values and norms that you have internalised from, say, media sources or your family background may assist you to act and speak more consistently with who you truly are. There are numerous books, tapes and courses that assist this process of reframing and remoulding your beliefs, if you choose or feel the need.

In my experience, speaking assertively, that is, taking time to own your own statements and saying 'I . . .', will assist you to get in touch with what you believe or want. In other words, making a start on 'I statements' is very helpful in helping you determine your 'whats'.

The final stage of being assertive is taking *action* yourself to have your own needs met. Often this involves you needing to act by yourself, or to find other resources to ensure that you succeed in having your needs met. For some people this is difficult because they have been socialised into believing that they have to do things with their partner/friend and there is a discomfort in stepping outside a relationship to achieve an activity or a goal of interest to only one of the parties. Remember that whether you do or don't act—you live with the ' consequences. There is no way around this. Even if you choose to do *nothing*, then *that* is still a choice. It's a choice not to choose (and again, you live with the consequences).

41

As a result, I suggest that you learn to be more effective and achieve more 'wins' for yourself (without making other people lose) rather than allowing events to just happen to you. Acting assertively is about taking charge of your life, empowering yourself with choice, and accepting the consequences of such choice.

If you feel 'merged' (co-dependent) with another person and have difficulty in taking action when the other party doesn't approve and won't accompany you or help, you might like to consider raising your consciousness about the nature of relationships, and the possibilities available in relationships.

Figure 2.7 outlines three different relationship types. Model (A) is characterised by the idea that now that We are together we are mainly Us with a little bit of I left over and a little bit of You left over. Figure model (B) indicates that now that we are together there is a small amount of We / Us, You are largely You and I am still predominantly I or Me. Figure model (C) is characterised by the idea that I am Me and can never be You and am quite separate from you, You are never able to be me and our boundaries are delineators of our separateness. Notice the 'merged boundaries' in models (A) and (B).

Much of the relatively recent 'recovery' work being offered to victims of abuse in primary relationships (family of origin, marriage, parenting etc.) centres around the issue of 'poor' or 'damaged' boundaries. People are being asked to consider how their patterns of abuse are being lived out in present relationships that are overly merged or 'co-dependent'.

I don't believe that one of the relationships in Figure

Figure 2.7: Three styles of relationships

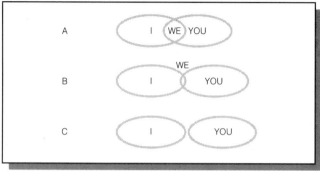

2.7 is the 'best'. I have observed that people often appear
to live most happily together as long as they believe in
the same style, or combinations of style of relationship.
Problems often arise when one party believes more in
(B) for example and the other party is more attracted
to (A) as their understanding of how things 'should' be.

Many couples' therapists believe that the healthiest
style of relationship is one where there can be merging
of boundaries at times when it suits both parties and an
independence or separation of boundaries at other times.
This can be as simple as:

> 'Tonight I want to be with you watching television and
> snuggling up on the couch but tomorrow I want to have
> the day to myself. I'm going to a course with friends.'

Difficulties often arise when we try to negotiate our
needs and attempt to satisfy the requirements of both
parties—to deal with your 'whats' at the same time as
satisfying my differing 'whats'. For this we need an
assertive problem-solving approach and *assertive* interper-

43

sonal skills so that we can work out a solution where we both 'win'; that is, achieve our needs and share 'power'.

Isn't this all too difficult?

I don't believe so. I don't think it is too difficult to understand the basic differences between *passive*, *aggressive* and *assertive* communication, the need for *working out your values* and being prepared *to act* and adjust your speech patterns. My teaching experience with thousands of learners has been that learning to speak with assertive 'I statements' is relatively simple and is usually achieved the same day as the person attending the course decides they want to trial this slight but significant difference in speaking.

Many people report that within a day they have become very aware of other people using broad speaking 'You statements'. Within a day or two people find themselves adjusting their own sentences. They begin to speak by saying:

'You now how you . . .' *and then adjust it to* 'I have found that I have . . .'

When I meet people a year or two after an assertion program they report they are consistently owning their own statements and using 'I . . .' Indeed, I can hear this myself as they talk to me.

If you are interested in changing your aggressive or passive patterns into assertion you are likely to achieve this with a small amount of initial effort. If you don't choose to do so that is still okay. That is your position

44

on the matter and you live with the consequences of that choice.

Our cultural norms, being set in 'power-over'/win–lose, prevent development of assertive communication. As Chapters 1 and 2 indicate, being non-assertive may be the 'norm' but this isn't necessarily going to be fair for you. I believe we live in an oppressive and unjust society that has a variety of ways to perpetuate losers who are disadvantaged by the systems, structures, norms and rituals in their work and home institutions. One of the most significant ways of perpetuating lack of power in the individual is to continue the distorted and flawed communication techniques that are common in this culture; that is, non-assertive ways of speaking and listening.

Assertion, because it is about collaborative, co-operative action and belief, disturbs the cultural patterns of patriarchy, power over others, absolutes or 'truths', labelling people as in or out, and consequent damaged self-esteem.

Assertion is a very useful technique for you to employ to empower yourself in relation to your environment. In addition, its use disrupts our societal habits and has a powerful effect in changing our culture.

Basic guidelines for communication

The following represents eleven tips on the do's and don'ts of assertive communication. As you go through each point you will probably recognise some habits. It may become apparent there is a certain theme running through your patterns; that is, you may have a habit of frequently using some aggressive techniques in your interactions. This section is designed to help you become aware of any strong patterns you may have been using in the past as well as to introduce you to realising *ineffective* communication styles in yourself and others. You will notice many of these guidelines go against the 'norm' of what you may have been taught or led to believe was 'okay' in the past. Allow yourself the opportunity to reconsider your previous points of view and perhaps take on some new ways of seeing your interpersonal interactions.

1   *Say 'I'* when you are expressing something that you think or feel or have done instead of using words like 'you', 'they', 'people'. Thus you acknowledge that what you are saying is about you, and thereby let people get to know you.

This is *assertive* communication.

2   *Don't rescue*, which is doing for someone what they can do for themself. This is a discount of the other person because you are acting as if they can't take care of themself.

If Mary and Sue are discussing something or arguing with each other and I step in and say 'Mary I think you are being a bit harsh on Sue' or I say 'What Sue is trying to say is . . .' that is rescuing.

You may have been taught that this is a helpful or 'kind' technique of support—it is *rescuing* somebody and sending a clear message to everybody in that interaction that you think you can handle this better than Sue. If Sue is a staff member or child of yours it may be that she never develops confidence and competence to deal with situations herself. For

Mary, who is now facing two people against her, it can appear overwhelming and often generates feelings of tension and *aggressive/passive* reactions in the person in this situation.

Another typical example of rescuing occurs in work situations where, in a meeting, somebody will finish off the point of view or sentence of another party. If you are someone who likes to be rescued you will actually ask somebody else to be on your side, or to agree with you, or to complete what you were saying, and will thank people for having rescued you.

How could you make a comment on a topic you are interested in without falling into the category of rescuing?

There are a number of ways, including asking the two people engaged in debate if it is suitable for you to comment: 'I'd like to express my point of view on this—is that okay?' (Bear in mind one or both parties may tell you that it is not okay—that they are in fact having enough difficulty just dealing with each other without an additional person or point of view.) Another option is to assert your point of view with 'I think . . .' followed by your opinion as opposed to your agreement or disagreement with someone else's point of view. Alternatively, you can stay out of the interaction, allowing people to sort out the situation themselves. Managers and parents often believe their employee or child will benefit more from being allowed to be responsible for the situation rather than being 'helped'.

Rescuing is *I win–you lose* and is therefore *aggressive*.

3   *Avoid interpreting.* An interpretation is when you tell someone what motivates them, why they feel, think or act the way they do. For example, 'You are an angry person.' The main reason this is not a good way to communicate is that the other person probably will feel defensive. This is because you are labelling or diagnosing the person which implies that they have a problem and you are superior enough to be able to see and name it. A win–lose dynamic is set up.

It's much more effective and straightforward to tell the person how you feel or describe what it is that makes you think as you do, for example, 'I notice that you argue and disagree with most of the things I have said and it's hard for me to talk to you.' Here you're describing what you think and feel and owning it yourself.

Later in this chapter you will learn a useful, powerful formula for telling a person that their behaviour is unacceptable to you and that you would like them to change. It is very important that you describe *behaviour* (not the person) and what it's like for *you* instead of the problem that *they have*.

Can you see the difference between you owning the problem and your blaming the other person?

Interpreting is *I win–you lose* and is therefore *aggressive*.

4   *Feelings* and *thoughts* are different, although we often confuse the two in language. For instance, 'I feel that you are wrong' is a thought, not a feeling. Use 'I feel

ASSERTION

'. . .' only when expressing feelings (anger, sadness, fear, happiness, fatigue, and so on). Be specific and clear in your communication.

Apart from the use of 'I feel' in the example above ('I feel that you are wrong about that'), what else do you notice that is non-assertive in the communication?

There are a couple of things—the word 'wrong' is a label or judgment. Words such as good, bad, correct, crazy, wrong, imply they lose–you win. Also of concern in that comment are the words 'I feel that you'. This is not an 'I statement' it is a 'you statement'. It is 'you are wrong about that' with an 'I feel' stuck on the front to disguise it. To say: 'I feel or think or believe "that you" . . .' is not assertive. 'That you' is a 'you' statement and carries with it judgment or blame.

This category of communication can be either *aggressive* or *passive*. It is not assertive.

5   *Confront* other people's behaviour, statements or mis-statements. Confrontation is a sign of caring. When you ignore or go along with someone's game-playing, discounting and so on you are hurting that person and acting as if you don't care. You can confront in a caring way without attacking the person or their behaviour.

I have noticed this is one of the hardest assertive skills for most people in our culture although it is one that is most often requested in training programs. It appears we need to have some techniques of confronting other people's behaviour, yet fear doing so. Many people report to me that they sense there

49

are 'games' going on between themselves and the people they are communicating with, or that the other people are not telling them something important.

For example, someone may appear quite miserable with a hangdog expression and speaking in a slow monotone while saying: 'I'm really looking forward to giving that speech, I think it's going to be great fun.'

Confronting involves you pointing out the discrepancy; for example, saying 'I hear you say that, yet I sense something else' or 'there is more to it than you are saying'. Confronting is also useful to point out to someone a pattern of theirs that you are aware of and you think they are not. There may be an employee who has a habit of saying they cannot help because they are too busy, there is not enough time, there is never enough time, time is a real problem, and so on. It can be helpful for your interaction if you point out to them 'I notice that you often talk about time, and not having any, in your conversations with me.'

To be able to confront people effectively you may need to lose your desire to be liked or to always have friendly, 'pleasant' interactions. Confrontation is taken by many people to be about attack. The way you are now learning to confront assertively is not about attack, it is about assertion and shows care and concern for the other person. Parents, supervisors and carers need to use this skill often to keep communication open and honest. You may find some people will thank you after you have bothered to confront them because you have made them think about something they may have been avoiding.

Confrontation is *assertive*.

6 *Take responsibility* for how you feel, think and behave. Don't say 'You make me angry' because that makes your feelings someone else's responsibility. Instead say 'I am angry because . . .' (and state your reasons). Avoid saying 'makes me feel'.

A little later in the chapter I will ask you to consider a formula that requires you to *describe* the behaviour that has bothered you:

'When you speak to me in that tone of voice . . .'
and then *explain* how you feel
'I feel put down and angry.'

Taking responsibility for how you feel and think and behave is *assertive*.

7 *Avoid asking questions* unless you really require information. Often questions are an indirect way of making statements and a way of shifting responsibility onto someone else. For example: 'Don't you think that . . . ?' This is a sneaky way of making a statement without taking responsibility for it.

'Don't you think that . . .' is a closed question where you make a statement without owning it. In Chapter 4 when we look at the nature of questioning you will find that such closed questions do not build rapport between people and, in fact, can have the opposite effect. If you want to make a point, own it honestly by saying 'I think that . . .' as opposed to trying to get someone to agree with you or see things your way.

A useful way to deal with somebody who uses closed questions with you is to assert yourself by commenting on their style of communication: 'I hear you asking me a question and yet I sense you really have an opinion of your own. What is it?' They may answer that they were only asking a question and have no opinion at all. Try restating that you think they do (have an opinion) and you would like to hear what it is they think on the topic. Alternatively, you may prefer to sum up their point of view—'sounds like you think X on this' (they will have told you all about X after having stated 'Don't you think that . . .')

Asking questions when you really are making a statement is *aggressive* or *passive*. It is not assertive.

8 *Avoid discounting*, which is acting as if what you think or feel is more important than what the other person thinks or feels. Discounting can also come in the form of denigrating yourself and acting as if the other person is more important than you.

Some examples of discounting are:

- interrupting—discounting the person who is talking. Many people say 'Oh, it's just that I was excited or I was keen. I didn't mean any harm in interrupting.' If you interrupt a person you send a clear message to them and anyone else listening that you think what you have to say is more important than what they have to say. This is win–lose or *aggressive* behaviour.

- not speaking because you think you'll sound stupid—self-discounting. An example of self-discounting is saying nothing, or 'I was going to say . . .' or 'This is only my opinion but . . .' You are entitled to your opinion and if you consider that there are no absolute right or wrong opinions—just different positions—you can afford to be comfortable about expressing your rights and views.

- not taking the other person's desires into account. For example, deciding what you will do on a date—discounting the other person. Any time you assume your needs are more important or your views are the views of your team, family, partner, children—the boundaries of yourself and others merge, and it is not possible for other people to have their position. This is where you win–they lose. It is therefore *aggressive*. It is for this reason that the word 'we' is often so unhelpful in communication. Consider this, 'We don't like to go to the beach. We much prefer the mountains, don't *we* darling.'
- saying things that put yourself down. This is self-discounting. *Passive* behaviour includes habits such as 'I'm hopeless at this' or 'Watch me muck this up' or 'I'm never going to get this right.'

9 *Avoid using exaggerations* or exaggerated words such as 'always', 'never', 'incredible', 'the most . . . in the world' and so on. This is often a way of justifying your ineffectiveness, avoiding a problem, or avoiding responsibility for your behaviour. For example, 'I was so angry, I couldn't help myself.' The fact is that you could help yourself.

Swearing also can come into this style of communication. If you use swear words often in your common conversation you may be losing clarity in expressing what you think.

Being assertive does not preclude swearing and in the next section you are going to look at how you can maintain some of your usual habits (including swearing if that is your style) without being aggressive.

Use of exaggeration is *aggressive* or *passive*.

10 *Avoid qualifying statements* or phrases such as 'perhaps' and 'maybe' unless you are really unsure. Such words are often a way of avoiding responsibility for what you say.

Likewise 'try' is often used as a way of really saying 'I won't do it'. Trying is very different from *doing*. If you have someone in your life who is going to 'try to remember to be more assertive' you might like to confront that and tell them that you don't want them to try you actually would like them to *do* it.

Avoiding responsibilities is *passive communication*.

11 *Avoid such statements* as 'I can't' and 'I have to' unless that is really the case. It is rare that we are unable or incapable of doing something and rarely true that we 'have to' do anything unless someone is physically forcing us. The truth is that in most cases we choose to act the way we do, because otherwise we would suffer unpleasant consequences.

Attributing external control is *passive* communication.

IN SUMMARY

To be assertive, you . . .

	1	need to know *what*	—you value
			—you need
			—you want
and	2	*tell* others about	—your thoughts
			—your feelings
			—yourself
and	3	initiate *action* to get your needs met.	

Assertiveness is communicating and acting *honestly* and *directly*. You stand up for *your rights* in a way that does *not* violate the other person's rights or stop them meeting their needs.

The essence of assertion is using 'I statements'.

An 'I statement' is *owning* your ideas, needs and opinions. For example: 'I like being with my family.'

It does not include your interpretation or evaluation. For example: 'It's good to spend time with your family,' or 'You have to spend time with your family.'

An 'I . . .' message is honest and congruent. It shows the real extent of your thoughts and feelings. It is clear, understandable and to the point. For example: 'I feel put down when you say that.'

It is *not* vague or roundabout-ish. For example: 'I guess I maybe feeling slightly annoyed.'

The four types of 'I statements'

'I statements' are appropriate for all purposes ranging from stating your opinion to what is often difficult for many people—confronting someone whose behaviour is unacceptable to you. 'I statements' are critical tools in changing to *power-with* styles of relationship.

Type 1: Stating
To state something about yourself (your thoughts or feelings).

Some examples: 'I like to have time alone.'
'I feel angry about it.'
'It seems to me to work.'
'I believe in it.'

Type 2: Answering
This is where you say yes or no to a request from another person and follow it with some sort of a *stating* 'I statement'. (You may or may not choose to give much detail or explanation.)

Some examples: 'Yes, I would like to join you in that.'
'No, I don't want to get involved in that group.'
'I have other things I need to do.'
'No, I don't want to give money for that project.'

Type 3: Preventing
This is where you tell another person of your needs in order to prevent potential future conflict. It is also where you alert another person of an action that you have decided to take or ask them for their help in order for you to meet your needs. (Remember, they can decline to assist you—that is their right.)

An example: 'I need to set up the meetings for Wednesdays. What times suit you best?'

Notice that the day for the meetings is not negotiable in this—however, the time is. It's important that you work out your position on the matter (if there are areas for negotiation).

'I have decided to get fitter and I will go to the gym twice a week.'

(Notice how different this statement is from 'Do you mind if I go to the gym a couple of times each week'. This statement would be assertive only if you truly were interested in their opinion and required their permission.)

If you have decided to take the action you need to state it as such. If you are open to discussion on the details of how and when the action will take place, then say so: 'I have decided to go to the gym twice a week. What times would be most convenient for you?'

Another example: 'I really want to improve my computer skills. Can you help me with some coaching on this?'

Please note that the other person has the same right as you and is allowed to decline if it is not one of their needs or wants.

You, in turn, have the right to ask a second time, perhaps giving more details or being more specific on what you wish from them. To continuously repeat your request is harping and denying their right to have different 'wants' from you.

Type 4: Confronting
Confronting is telling another person that you cannot

accept their behaviour because it interferes with one or more of your needs.

Some examples: 'When you don't keep deadlines, I feel very angry with you.'

'When you play your music this loud, I can't concentrate on what I am doing. I'm feeling frustrated.'

'When you say that, I feel put down and ignored.'

Please note that each of these confrontative 'I statements' commence with a *when* . . . followed by description of behaviour.

For many people, simply describing the behaviour and then explaining how you feel (as above), is enough to raise their awareness, and encourage an immediate change from them. Some people however, will need the *full four-part confrontative 'I statement'* (DESC).

The full four-part confrontative 'I statement' (DESC)

D Describe the situation or behaviour: 'When you . . .' (don't judge/blame)

E Explain how you feel, what you think: 'I feel / I believe . . .'

S Suggest an alternative: 'I need / I would prefer / I want . . .'

C Consequences—state the benefits: 'So that / in order that . . .'

For example: If you have interrupted me, I may say:

'When you interrupt before I have finished saying what I need to, I feel frustrated.'

If this situation has occurred a couple of times I may prefer to use the full DESC:

'When you interrupt me, I feel frustrated. I need you to let me finish before you begin to speak so that I feel I'm surviving equally in the conversation.'

So—where to from here?

Change Agents (teachers, counsellors, industry consultants etc.) have known for a long time that insight doesn't necessarily create change. In other words, just because you now have a better understanding of the principles of assertion, it doesn't follow necessarily that you will be able to use them unless you *practise*. At this point, many readers may choose to turn to the next chapter to move onto the next set of theories. Don't. *Do the exercises first.*

Many participants in my training courses who have asked for practical skills say that they are not comfortable to do exercises and role plays. Let me be quite clear on *my* position on this. I firmly believe:

You cannot gain skills unless you practise.

It is not possible for you to become a *practitioner* of *skills* by reading my information or listening to a tape on the topic. Skills are about you *doing*, not just reading or listening. If you are seriously interested in becoming a more effective/assertive communicator, you need to do at least some of the exercises that will be outlined for you. None of them are long, and they will give you the practical confidence to use these techniques in your life, which is, after all, what most people want, and why they are attracted to courses and books of this kind.

EXERCISES

Exercises to practise stating 'I statements'
Here are two exercises that require you to write your answers to the response (allowing you to revise what you have written and look for any non-assertive areas) and two that are verbal responses. Do the written ones first.

Exercise 1
What do you think of the current Prime Minister's performance in government? (Now *write* your assertive answer in as much detail as you would like. *Write* it as if you were going to say this out loud to somebody who has asked you the question.)

Exercise 2
What do you think of this book so far? (*Write* your answer in as much detail as you can, being assertive in stating your opinion.)

Exercise 3
Do this exercise and Exercise 4 verbally, that is, *speak* out loud as if you are answering somebody who has just asked you the question. Listen to your response and, if necessary, correct yourself any time you are not being assertive.

What do you think about the idea that feminism has a lot to offer our society?

Exercise 4
Why do you think so many people are interested in improving their interpersonal communication skills?

FEEDBACK

Type 1—Stating

To check how well you are progressing in being fully assertive, you can either ask someone else to look over what you have written and 'hear' your responses to *Type 1 (Stating) 'I statements'* or you can go back over the material yourself using the Basic Guidelines For Communications section on pages 45–54.

The general rule of thumb for whether or not you are being assertive is as follows:

> Did you own your own statements ('I think', 'I have found' and 'I put') or did you fall into the habit of saying 'we', 'you' or 'most people'? Remember, you can speak only for yourself, and any time you use broad generalisations, sweeping statements, or bring other people's opinions into your argument, you are being non-assertive. Some examples are:
>
> 'I don't agree with the Prime Minister's views on Education and Health funding.' *(Assertive)*
>
> as opposed to:
>
> 'I think that he should improve his policy on Education and Health.' *(Non-assertive)*

Notice why this is not assertive. 'He should', with an 'I think' put on the front of it is *not* assertive. Assertive would be 'I would prefer to see him attend to . . .' or 'I don't like . . .'

Words like should, must, have to, ought, are *not* assertive as they assume a superior position (I win–you lose). Similarly, words like good, bad, right, wrong ('I think you are wrong about that') are *not assertive*.

Similarly, 'I think that most people will get a lot out

of this book' is *not* assertive. You can not speak for most or all people unless you have just done a huge survey and have their permission to speak for them. Speak for yourself.

'I am gaining things from this book.'

With regard to the question on feminism, answers such as:

'One tends to feel that feminism is overstating itself with regard to applications in management, human relations, and survival of the planet' are *not assertive.*

This statement appears to have been delivered from the lofty heights of a god's eye perspective—as an absolute truth. You can speak only from your own experience and opinion. So own it yourself:

'I find that feminism overstates its principles' is *assertive.*
'To me its application in areas of management, human relations, and planetary survival is hard to follow' is *assertive.*

Exercises to practise answering 'I statements'

Type 2—Answering
In these exercises I would like you to give a Yes or No answer first, so decide on your '*what*' before you begin and be honest about whether you do or don't want to say 'Yes' to the request. As in exercises for Type 1, I suggest you do the first two in *written* form so that you can revise what you have written and look for areas of non-assertion. Do the second two exercises verbally and 'out loud'.

1   Would you like to come to a two-hour meeting next

Thursday night at the City Hall? It is on communication skills to enhance personal growth. (Work out
your stance on this position and then give as detailed
an answer as you choose to.)

2 I'm fundraising for the Women's Domestic Violence
   Centre. Can you contribute to the fund, please?
   (Write your answer being fully assertive about your
   position.)

3 (Do this one out loud.) Imagine your boss has come
   up to you and said, 'We are keen for all staff to
   become more actively involved in public relations
   activities with prospective clients. Are you prepared
   to get involved in this? (Remember, you may have
   more than one 'what', you may also have some
   provisos—it is your choice.)

4 (State your response out loud.) I'd really like you to
   help me with this problem. Can you give me some
   time? (This is often one of the most difficult situations for many people, particularly women, to refuse.
   I have left it a broad request. I would like you to
   imagine a scenario, choose what sort of help it would
   be and answer Yes or No to the request.)

Now go back over your written answers and your verbal
responses to check for full assertion. It may be necessary
to read the chapter's theory again, particularly sections
on assertive vs aggressive and passive in order to reconsider your answers.

Type 3—Preventing
The first two exercises need to be written, the second
two may be done verbally and 'on the spot'.

1 A new employee appears to have more latitude and responsibility than you. You believe you are at least equal in qualifications and experience. You are concerned you may be undervalued and perhaps, under-utilised. Approach your superior with your concerns. (*Write* your answer as though you were speaking to your superior.)

2 You have been passed over for a promotion but no reasons were given. The interview seemed to go well and you believe you were the most suitable candidate. You would like some more details about the situation and your chances for future advancement. You have decided to approach your senior manager for some answers. (*Write* your answer in dialogue form.)

3 (Verbal response.) Tell your partner/friend/spouse of a need of yours or an action you have decided you are going to take in the area of your own self-improvement. Choose a personal goal, or something you have always wanted to set as a goal, and explain in detail what you are going to do (and even why, if you choose to disclose those details).

4 (Verbal response.) Imagine you are approaching a colleague or boss and you are wanting to let them know one or more of your needs in the job. You would like their support/help, in order for you to meet your needs.

Type 4—Confronting
For the following exercises *write* out a full DESC response using the process on pages 58–59. **D**: Remember to describe the behaviour, not the person, and be quite

specific about exactly what they are doing that you believe is unacceptable or violating your rights. **E**: Be honest about how you feel. **S**: State what it is you need or prefer, in as much detail as you can. **C**: And wherever possible, give consequences that are beneficial to both of you. If this is not possible, give the benefits to yourself.

1 Your friend has a habit of putting you down in a joking manner in front of other people, you have had enough of this and believe it is affecting other people's opinion of you. (*Write* out your DESC as if you were saying it to the person.)

2 Your boss has asked you to investigate an issue and hasn't given you enough time to do it justice. This situation is occurring often. Confront your boss. (*Write* out your reply as if you were saying it.)

3 A member of your staff jokes all the time. You find it difficult to understand what he really means and can't tell if he understands you. (DESC the staff member.)

Now try the following role-playing exercises *verbally*, doing the DESC out loud. Take your time. You don't have to speak quickly. The other person often hears you out, as long as you stay assertive.

4 You have moved into a new neighbourhood, and need to speak to a neighbour who allows their children to use part of your yard as their cricket field. You have asserted that you are not happy with this and wish to use the garden yourself. Your neighbour has replied: 'We're all pretty friendly around here, love. We don't tend to worry about this sort of

thing—boundaries and so on. You should relax a little bit more. They are only just kids having fun.' Confront the neighbour with how inappropriate you find their reply and state what it is you require. (You can choose any or all aspects of the neighbour's reply, it is up to you.)

5 You are talking with a person who has called you 'love/matey/dear' three or four times in the last few minutes. You barely know this person and have not given them permission to address you in this way. Confront the person.

6 Choose a situation from your recent past, where you felt you have not dealt assertively with a person or situation. Convert it now into an appropriate confrontative 'I statement' using the full DESC steps.

Now go back over what you have written and said, and look for where you have been fully assertive and where you have become passive or aggressive. Remember, it is important to describe the behaviour:

> for example, 'when you speak to me in that tone of voice', (*Assertive*)
> and *not* label or judge the person
> for example, 'when you are rude and inconsiderate'. (*Non-assertive*)

The latter style of communication, being aggressive, will cause reaction in the listener and they are unlikely to let you go further in your statement. What is more likely to occur is that they will get you into 'quicksand' by arguing backwards and forwards:

> 'I was not rude', 'Yes you were', 'No I wasn't' etc.

66

Check that you have been honest about how you feel and that it is not a 'tirade'. While it is appropriate to give a *couple* of feelings or thoughts, it is not assertive to take up all of the air space with a lengthy list of arguments. For example:

'I feel angry and frustrated'
'and furthermore'
'I'm sick of the number of times it is happening, and also, I remember you did this to me last Christmas and . . .'

It is much more straightforward to say:

'I feel angry and I remember how many times it has previously happened.' (*Assertive*)

For the stating of your preferred alternative behaviour, the more specific you can be, the better. For example:

'I'd like you to improve your attitude'

is *not very clear*. What this means could be easily debated and even misunderstood. Be quite specific by what you mean, for example:

'I'd like you to look at me and appear to listen when I'm speaking to you.' (*Assertive*)

or

'I'd like you not to roll your eyes and sigh at me as I am speaking.' (*Assertive*)

It's preferable to mention the positive behaviour you are looking for, as opposed to asking the person to stop the negative.

Be careful not to become aggressive on the last stage

of the DESC as you are stating consequences. For example:

> 'When you speak to me in that tone of voice I feel annoyed. I'd like you to stop it so that you can leave the room with both your legs intact',

may be somewhat amusing in the reading but is actually aggressive! Becoming aggressive or sarcastic on the last comment will lose the power and influence you have gained in first part of your 'I . . .' message.

Final exercise

I want you to imagine that someone has just looked over your shoulder while you are reading this book and has made the following statement: 'Don't you think these books are only for people who have got some sort of psychological problem? Don't you reckon you'd be better off not worrying about this kind of stuff and just having more fun in life? Your problem is you tend to take everything too seriously, and you end up with a chip on your shoulder.'

Out loud and off the top of your head, confront this imaginary person, using the full DESC formula. Choose to object to any, or all, aspects of what they have said.

For example, you may choose to confront *only one* of the specific comments made:

> 'When you tell me not to worry about this "stuff" I think you are making judgments about how I should live my life.'
> 'I wish to develop my own views on psychology (and you are entitled to yours) so then we can each work on our own philosophy of life.'

68

Alternatively, you may prefer to deal with the 'gist' of the story you are hearing. (To paraphrase or sum up the main ideas of the story, be careful not to 'go too far' in analysis of what was said or become aggressive in retaliation.)

'When you imply there is something wrong with me, or what I'm doing, I think you overstep my boundaries.'

'I need to do what I think is important for me, so that I can develop better understanding of myself and others.'

Some examples of non-assertive DESCs

See if you can pick the non-assertion in each of these:

Example 1

'When you say I'm crazy, I feel upset.. I need you to be more considerate and helpful, so that we can get on better.'

Can you *see/hear* the non-assertive parts?
Here they are:

When you say I'm *crazy*	(a judgment/label/ diagnosis = *Aggressive*)
I feel upset	(*is assertive*, unless upset is an understatement of how mad, furious etc. you really are = *Passive*)
I need you to be more *considerate* and *helpful*	(implies the person is *inconsiderate* and *unhelpful* = *Aggressive*)

| So that *we* can get on better | (speak for yourself and do not assume there is a '*we*' or that they wish to get on with you at all = *Aggressive/Passive*) |

How could this be improved and made fully assertive?

Example 2
What's *non-assertive* here?

'When you tell me not to worry about this psychological mumbo-jumbo, I feel that you are being very analytical yourself. I would prefer you didn't do this so I can remain friends with you.'

Where are the *non-assertive* parts?
Here they are:

| When you tell me not to worry about this *psychological mumbo-jumbo* | (they can argue that they did not use these words. You have over-interpreted their point and haven't stayed with observable verifiable behaviour— *aggressive*) |

| I feel that *you are* being very *analytical* yourself | (any time you use 'you are' even if 'I feel' is beforehand, you are blaming or judging. Analytical is a label— *aggressive*) |

I would prefer you didn't do this	is *assertive*
So I can *remain friends with you*	this is a threat. If you don't get your own way you will withdraw yourself—payback—*aggressive*

How could this be improved on and made fully assertive?

PRESCRIPTIONS

In therapy or professional development training a prescription is where the counsellor/teacher suggests you practise some new behaviour. This means having a go at doing something *different* or doing the same things as usual but in a different way.

My prescription for you is: *on a number of occasions each day make a conscious effort to speak assertively to another person or persons.* Within a very short time, assertive speaking becomes habit as opposed to something you have to concentrate on. This will happen only with some practise.

This chapter, indeed the entire book, may show you that you have a habit of catching with your *right hand*, metaphorically speaking. The way to learn to become your potential is to deliberately practise *left-handed* catching. That way you end up with your old pattern which you know, (right-handed catching), some new skills (left-handed catching, two-handed catching) and another game—I'm not catching at all, I don't want to play.

To develop this range of skills, you need to stop catching only right-handed for a short time. It is important you develop left-handed catching by systematically applying and practising the new skill.

Enjoy the experience of changing and learning over the next few days.

3
The Other Side of Being Assertive— Listening Skills

I LISTEN OKAY, DON'T I?

In my experience many of us do not really listen. Some of us have habits of listening in to some parts of the conversation whilst having our mind wander for periods of time. Some tend to listen to gather only enough information to argue back. Others listen rather judgmentally and constantly analyse what the person is saying to try to 'figure them out'.

Just as societal norms and culture mould the individual into adhering to certain value and belief systems, the communication habits of our environment affect the way many of us learn to speak and listen.

You may recognise in Figure 3.1 some of the 'scripts' that you have been living out. You were probably conditioned by your significant life experiences at home, school and work. For example, you may have had family role models who won arguments and needed to take control. This is often the case if you have been socialised in a fairly traditional male sex role. Many females are over-socialised in terms of serving others, in being liked and in being 'feminine'. This is often about allowing yourself to be beaten by others.

Some of us (female or male) don't listen because we are in a rush to speak, to prove our point and to win the discussion. Alternatively, we may be trying to avoid conflict so we do anything to sidestep admitting there is a problem that needs resolving.

The communication habits of our culture are a tremendous influence on each of us as individuals—even if we consciously have not noticed this. The skills

Figure 3.1: Societal norms of communication

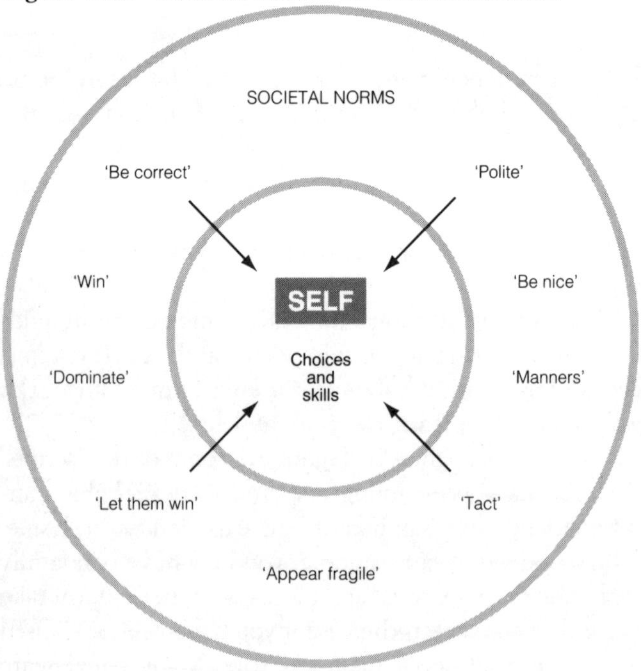

SOCIETAL NORMS

'Be correct'   'Polite'

'Win'   'Be nice'

SELF
Choices
and
skills

'Dominate'   'Manners'

'Let them win'   'Tact'

'Appear fragile'

presented in this chapter will enhance your choices and give you a range of techniques you can use to better understand another human being. Listening is about attending to another person's needs. It doesn't mean you have to agree with them or even like them. It's about being prepared to understand, tolerate, or even care for, another person by being able to hear them.

Assertive listening is the other part of using *power-with* communication. It serves as an antidote to *power-over* styles of relating.

As you work your way through this chapter you may on some occasions be asking the question 'but when do I get to say what *I* think?' In order to learn the listening skills thoroughly, this chapter focuses only on the right-hand side of Figure 2.1 on page 30. Listening skills, in reality, do not go by themselves. They are part of the ebb and flow (the speaking and listening) of communicating with another person. For the sake of learning the skills, however, they are presented in seeming isolation from 'I statements'.

In the next chapter, the two sides of communicating will be put back together, strategically and in a particular order, to encompass the advanced interpersonal abilities of handling resistance and influencing.

WHY BOTHER LEARNING NEW LISTENING SKILLS?

I believe there are a number of very good reasons for most of us to reclaim some assertive listening habits or to completely change some of the techniques that we have been bringing to our relationships. For a start, if you are interested in the interpersonal skills required for consulting, selling, negotiating, managing and problem solving you need advanced techniques of speaking and listening to overcome resistance and solve conflict. In order to do the advanced skills (found in Chapter 4), the skills of both speaking and listening assertively are prerequisite.

You simply can't do the advanced skills work unless you are a true practitioner of some of the more crucial 'basics'. For example, to be able to settle down an irate person to the point where the two of you can look at possible solutions for solving the problem, you need to be able to use active listening, open questions and summarise their point of view before you assertively state your opinion or even confront them (see 'DESC'— on pages 58–59). The details of how to do this and the exercises to give you confidence and competence in these more advanced applications of communication will be dealt with in the next chapter.

Another reason to become an assertive listener is to disturb our cultural habits of *power-over* others. Listening is about shared power—*power-with*.

Caring for someone

To my mind, another reason for learning to listen is to show your care and concern for people you are in relationships with. Many of us need to use counselling skills for our children and our friends, and some of us act as coaches and therapists in our work lives. Many people reading this book are likely to need to counsel staff on work-related or personal issues. It is not particularly useful to just *tell* people what to do. This is simply *advice* as to what you think their solutions ought to be. This sets up win–lose dynamics of power over others and, when people are not empowered, they tend not to feel capable. They also tend not to act on solving problems. Listening skills provide us with some useful solutions for how to truly assist people to solve their own problems.

Listening is a sign of caring. When you listen carefully to another person you are sending a clear message that they are the total focus of your attention. It is a real privilege for a human being to be heard and understood and is a powerful ingredient in building a relationship of trust and rapport between two people. There are sure to be people in your personal life who would greatly appreciate your attention and your understanding of their point of view.

Remember, though, that this does not mean that you have to agree with them or see things their way. You are entitled to your own opinions and views, although you are listening to another person's perspective. We can listen without being beaten. There are other ways to live our lives besides win–lose dynamics and assertive listening techniques are a true example of this.

Using listening skills at work

In recent years in *industry training*, another rather pressing reason for learning listening skills has evolved. In Chapter 1, I mentioned some of the pressures on our workforce to *culturally* change. I discussed the shift away from merely being procedurally and technically competent in work, towards being much better at the people skills of relating to colleagues, staff, clients and bosses on a daily basis.

Quite simply, people who are not good listeners and

don't exhibit skills of being able to tolerate and accept other people's viewpoints are being seen as limited in their range of abilities and talents. As our society moves away from absolute and dogmatic beliefs towards multiple realities and consideration of various positions and their consequences, people who continue to talk as if theirs is the only opinion, who do not seek other views and do not listen with understanding to others, are losing career ground.

Our workplace cultures are moving away from passive and aggressive modes of communication towards problem solving that is collaborative and win–win. Listening is at least half of what's needed in working towards this vision.

If you haven't already read the information in Chapter 1 on workplace reform, culture change and social justice reforms, I suggest that you do so now in order to gain some 'macro' perspective on the 'micro' skills being covered in this chapter.

THE STEPS IN ACTIVE LISTENING

I will cover each of the steps of responding to another human being in the order that they tend to naturally occur. These steps, when put together in this same order, become a helping or counselling process. Each individual skill involved in attending to another human being is, however, immensely useful in its own right. The following stages are a very useful design for you to help people focus on their needs and the solutions they can activate to meet those needs.

In order to highlight each of the stages of listening to another person, I'm going to 'blow them up'—use a technique in which you experience them as somewhat larger than life. They will also appear as more separate from other parts of listening than they really are.

Step 1 of listening

In order to experience the first step of listening, imagine that you are listening to somebody telling you their story about a minor car accident they were involved in this morning on their way to work. Imagine they have just begun to tell you about what happened to them and that they are quite keen to tell you. Visualise this person in front of you. See them in your mind's eye and hear them beginning to talk. What would they be likely to say to you?

Now, your role is to listen—really listen. By this I mean you're to try to understand their issues and feelings almost as well as they do. One more thing—you are not allowed to speak to them. You cannot say anything. You are simply to give them the total focus of your attention. (The reason why you can't speak is to highlight the first stage of listening, which is quite unlikely to involve you talking.)

Now, what sort of thing can you do to really attend to the other person? What can you do to show the talker that they have your attention? What can you do to encourage them to be comfortable to talk to you? What things might you do that would 'put them off', 'cause them to stop sharing with you and cause them to feel uncomfortable?

Before you read on, answer the questions above. Have in your mind at least three or four things that you believe probably make up good listening habits for the early stages of someone telling you something.

Step 1 is active listening

The first stage of active listening will involve you being quiet. It is very difficult to properly listen to another person while you are talking. Unfortunately, some of us have the habit of picking up one of the first things that another person has said and telling them *our story* of something similar that happened to us. For example, 'Oh I had an accident myself a couple of years ago and I had a lot of trouble getting my insurance claim accepted and I found that . . .' is not good listening. In fact, this kind of sharing of your issues can indicate to the other party that you are not really interested in their story. You are really caught up in your own agenda.

> So the first thing to do to enable you to attend to another human being is to *be quiet*.

It is also important that you remain mentally alert to enable you to respond to the other person. Many of us drift off in terms of paying attention. This can be a bad habit that needs adjusting. It is, at least in part, due to the brain's ability to process information faster than the other person can speak. This causes a discrepancy between the talker's time to tell the story and the time it takes for you to hear and understand it. With the leftover time periods many of us have developed a habit of switching off, or our mind wanders onto other subjects.

It is not surprising that many full-time therapists and counsellors who need to listen for a living tend to keep their sessions to between 45 minutes and one hour.

Concentrated listening is very tiring. It is, however, wonderful for the talker to be offered this service in positive regard and care.

So another part of Step 1 is giving concentrated *mental attention*.

Another part of connecting with the talker is to maintain eye contact. For many cultures (particularly Anglo-Saxon culture), unless the listener is looking at you, the talker is not convinced that they are truly 'with you'. If you let your eyes wander around the room or you only half turn to somebody (giving them one eye and one ear, as such), this can send an unconscious message of lack of attention. Early in conversation, eye contact may be too intense for either party. If you notice that the talker's eyes are moving away from you and they appear uncomfortable with your gaze, take your eyes off them for periods of time and you will find this will settle down into a comfortable eye-to-eye contact shortly thereafter.

Some cultures, including indigenous Australians, have a different perspective on eye contact. Direct gaze is seen as indicative of brazenness or lack of respect. Bear cultural differences in mind in your attempts to be a caring listener.

For most of us, *eye contact* is an important part of being heard.

Posture and non-verbals are also an important part of the message that is being received by the talker. This is called various things by different authors and teachers. I'm going to name it 'mirroring'—a word emphasised by neurolinguistic programmers. Mirroring is setting yourself up to appear more like the other person so that they receive an unconscious message of similarity between the two of you. This contributes to feeling relaxed and attracted to you. Mirroring is a deliberate technique of building rapport and a relationship with another person. It involves you mirroring their body posture, tone of voice, speed of speech, animation of hands and breathing.

If I want to send a message to you that I am like you, I will sit down and mirror your posture fairly closely. If you are sitting with your right leg crossed over your left and leaning back in the chair, I will take up the same or a very similar posture. As our encounter (or counselling session) continues, if you change your posture to sitting forward with your hands on your knees and your legs uncrossed, I would follow shortly thereafter.

People do not notice this behaviour because it is a natural occurrence (except when you are deliberately practising it). The person to whom you are talking is unlikely to notice anything. Most will experience a vague sense of being at ease with you. You see, if you weren't trying to mirror the person it is quite likely it would occur anyway. People who are really attending to each other tend to mirror or mimic each other's rate of breathing, body stance and tone of voice. Think about two people who are very much in love. What do they look like? What do they sound like? Often they sound and look the same. Imagine yourself listening and talking with someone who is speaking slowly and quietly. When you speak, will you speak loudly? Quickly? Or will you join their world by communicating in a similar way?

Joining the other person—mirroring

Imagine yourself going into a room to pick up from the cot a wide awake, hot and unsettled baby. When you pick up that baby, do you pat it quickly or slowly? Most experienced people will say that you start off patting the child fast while walking briskly and *then* you start to slow down the patting and the walking. The child will slow down with you. Continued slowing of the patting may influence the child to sleep.

Here is an example of mirroring occurring naturally in someone who is trying to be empathic with another and/or influence that person. For some of us these techniques of joining the other person's world and leading them into our own come spontaneously. For others, we need to learn mirroring and to remember it each time we want to build rapport between ourselves and another person.

If you are thinking 'why should I bother to position my body in a way that suits another' and 'why should I adjust my rate or loudness of speech for another person who wants to talk differently from me', bear in mind that good listening is *not* about attending to *your needs*. It is about attending to the needs of the other party. If you can't, or won't do this, ask yourself 'What it is that stops me from being able to care in this way?' I have found that once someone tries mirroring a couple of times, they find for themselves the answers as to how hard it *really* is. Discover what kind of response you will receive.

You can imagine why barriers such as desks and folders are seen by many listening experts as totally inappropriate to developing a relationship with another person. Many managers do not talk with clients or staff across a desk any more. These days, many supervisors prefer to move round the desk and sit in similar chairs to enable an appropriate listening posture to be taken up.

The ability to adjust your style of posture, voice and gestures to that of the person talking is called *mirroring*.

Another crucial aspect to the first stage of listening to someone is to *nod your head* from time to time as you have understood and are following information. To accompany nods, you will often hear people murmuring 'uh huh', 'mmmm', 'yeah', 'right' and so on. These techniques are often termed 'minimal encouragers' and they have great effect in reassuring the listener that you're following them. I believe the best way to prove the effectiveness of this habit is for you to trial deliberately nodding your head as someone is speaking to you. See for yourself the positive feelings seemingly generated in the talker by this simple response from you. Try it today.

Making encouraging noises like 'uh-huh' is particularly important if you are using the telephone as part of your communication habits with people. No amount of your nodding to someone on the other end of the telephone will indicate to them that you are listening. For this medium, sound is imperative and never more imperative than with an upset or irate person.

Another part of Stage 1 is *nodding* and murmuring 'Uh huh'.

In summary, *Step 1* of active listening involves:

Being quiet	Mirroring
Mental concentration	Nodding
Eye contact	Uh-huh

Step 2 of listening

In order to draw out and highlight Step 2, imagine once again that you are listening to someone telling you a story about a car accident they had this morning. This time, you have been using the active listening techniques described above for some moments. The person has told you that they are worried that the accident may be seen as their fault, they may lose their no claim bonus, they are still feeling upset about it, and that their brand new car looks 'awful' with that dented metal.

Imagine the person is talking to you, try to hear the sort of thing they are saying and visualise this person as clearly as you are able. This time you can speak. You are able to communicate with them out aloud. What sort of thing can you say that will be helpful to the talker? What allows them to go where they want and what gets in their way? What forces them towards what you're interested in hearing?

Before you read on, formulate some answers to these questions in your mind.

Step 2 is open questions

You may already know the difference between open and closed questions and have some understanding of the differences in response that the two styles produce. It seems that many people learned something on this topic somewhere in a course at school or work.

For the purpose of this book I am going to define open questions as those which allow the talker to discuss whatever feelings, issues and points they are interested in. Closed questions are those which lead or direct the talker towards what the listener wants to figure out or hear about.

Closed questions

Although closed questions have their uses, they are not particularly helpful in building relationships and rapport. This is because closed questions focus on your need to figure out or solve the problem. Closed questions are often about asking for specific items of information; for example, 'What colour was the car?', 'Was it a man or woman driving?', 'How old are you?'

Other types of closed questions appear to be forcing the talker into 'yes' or 'no' answers; for example, 'Would you say that you could have been partly responsible?',

'Was the car yellow or not?' Other forms of closed questions seem to be about giving advice; for example, 'Don't you think it would have been better if you had . . .?', 'Would you say it was more a case of . . . or . . .?', 'Have you tried . . .?'

Many of us need to use closed questions in our work environments because we need to complete forms, gather specific information, obtain histories and so forth. While they have their usefulness in obtaining items of absolute information, they do not build good relationship dynamics between people. In fact, many people can become defensive about being quizzed in this way.

A number of health practitioners have told me that closed questions can often cause somebody to diagnose and figure out a medical problem 'too quickly'. Closed questions are often used by people who have already a strong sense of what 'the answer' is and are using these questions to narrow the person down to this answer. Again, this can cause misunderstanding or a reduced understanding of what actually occurred. Could it be that our culture, with its lust for certainty and the simple and its discomfort with the complexity of human possibilities, has taught us habits that limit our understanding of each other?

The alternative

Imagine the difference between asking somebody what they think of a topic and asking them if they think this or that? The first approach allows you and the other person to discover what they think as opposed to presuming there are a limited number of thoughts on the topic, with you checking to see which ones they adhere to.

Open questions are those which encourage the individual to explore their own realities. Commonly used open questions for this stage of listening include:

Problem-solving questions

1 Tell me more.
2 What's that about?
3 How was that for you?
4 How did you feel?
5 What's happening?
6 I'm not sure what you mean.
7 I'm not sure I completely understand.
8 Why (do you say that)?
9 What's your opinion?

When it is time to look at solutions use:

10 What have you tried?
11 What do you think you could do?
12 What options do you have?
13 What do you think you will do next?
14 So what are you going to do?

The use of open questions helps you to:

- join the other person's world completely
- allow the other person to focus on themselves
- better understand the other person
- help the other person to better understand themselves
- assist the other person to solve their own problems.

If you are interested in achieving any of these possibilities, it is time for you to start using open questions when listening to other people. Pick two or three from the left-hand column (numbers 1–9) and use them frequently over the next couple of days.

I tend to use 'Tell me more' and 'How do you feel about that?' When I am not following somebody's story very well, I also tend to use 'I'm not sure I understand what you mean.' Choose a couple of open questions that are most similar to the way you are comfortable speaking and overuse them to trial the effect they have on your relationships.

Remember, there is not a sign above your head saying 'Hey, I have just learned a technique called open questions and I'm using them on you'. Most people will not notice the particulars of what you are doing except that some people may comment to you that they find you a better listener, or 'more understanding' or 'changed somehow'. Personally, I don't see any reason why you can't share with somebody that you are working on changing or improving your interpersonal communication skills. I believe many people see this as admirable as opposed to anything to be mocked or scorned. Remember, the intent is to gain win–win solutions. Listening is about caring for other people's opinions.

Notice that open questions numbered 10–14 gently move the person to consider solutions to their problem. These questions are better used later in a conversation. If you use them too early it can sound like you don't care about the person and are trying to hurry them up. For example, 'How are you going?' followed a moment later by 'Well what are you going to do about it?' can leave the talker feeling not heard.

An exercise in using open questions

To give you some immediate practice in using open questions I am going to present myself to you as someone with a problem and I want you to use *only* open questions to listen and attempt to help me. Because you have just been introduced to open questions, please feel free to look them up to choose a suitable response. After a little while, if you think it is appropriate timing, try one of the open questions that focuses on solving the problem (numbers 10–14).

Just imagine I am telling you that I am not happy about something. To help you do the exercise, take a moment now to visualise what I may look like or sound like as I am talking to you. After each of my comments make your reply. Remember you are using *open questions* to do so. (Before you proceed you might like to cover the responses from 'You' I have included in the dialogue—work out your own reply first.)

ME: I am not very happy with my relationship with my brother.

YOU: (Choose an open question that you think will encourage me to talk to you and perhaps even solve my own problem.)

      Tell me more (or 'Go on' or 'I'm not sure I understand').

ME: Well, it has been going on for quite a while now and I am not very happy about it. I don't seem to be able to fix the situation.

YOU: *I'm not sure what you mean* (or 'Why do you say that?' or 'How do you feel about it?').

ME: He doesn't listen to what I'm saying and doesn't

seem to care about my life at all. He seems to live in his own world, mainly talking about his life and in particular his past. He never asks me about my life. In fact I have a sense when I'm with him that we have two different realities of what is going on at any given moment.

YOU: *How do you feel about that* (or 'What's that like for you?' or 'What happens for you?')?

ME: I feel very angry at times and at other times I'm hurt by his lack of connection with me. I've come to realise that he doesn't want real con- nections with people. He prefers to make up ones that are easier for him to deal with.

YOU: *What do you think you can do about this* (or 'What could you try?' or 'What options do you think you have?')?

ME: Well that's just it, I think I have tried just about everything that I'm prepared to and I really don't know what to do next. I have tried ignor- ing it on some occasions, other times I have confronted him about this, but nothing seems to have changed the way that he relates to me. At best, he interrupts me and doesn't ask me any questions about myself and, at worst, he rambles on and on and on about stories that are not connected to the present moment.

YOU: *What's that like for you* (or 'How do you feel when he does that?')?

ME: Look, I'm starting to get to the point where I think it's best for me if I don't care. I've tried all sorts of things over the years as have other people. Perhaps I need to stop trying and give myself permission to not feel responsible for sorting out a problem which after all may not be mine.

YOU: *Well, what do you think you will do next* (or 'What are you going to try?' or 'What will you do?')?

ME: Well, I think I'm going to work on not trying anything for a while. I'll just see how I feel about that. I'm going to try to stand back from myself a little and pay attention to what goes on between us without feeling that I've got to improve it.

Notice how using open questions, without any other skills or responses, is enough to give the person meaningful, caring assistance in being understood and solving their own problems. Open questions are an example of sharing power with others—feeling strong enough within yourself to be able to give another power to talk about whatever they choose.

Don't believe me though—try the skill out for yourself. The best way for any of us to find out what a skill will or will not achieve is to trial it for a period of time. Set it up a little like an experiment. On two or three occasions this evening use an open question with somebody and on two or three other occasions don't use an open question; in fact, use a closed one or even an assertive 'I statement'. Notice the difference in responses you get from the other party and pay attention to how you feel using the different techniques. Open questions can be a tremendous source of improved relationship dynamics between two people, but it is important that you test that out for yourself.

The problem with closed questions . . .

For those of us who have a strong and long-standing habit of excessively using closed questions, the following represents the same person with the same problem (me in relation to my brother) but the dialogue is altered this time with 'you' using closed questions or advice-giving responses. As you read through the dialogue, feel, see and hear the differences that are likely to occur for the talker as these less-appropriate responses are used.

ME: I am not very happy with my relationship with my brother.

YOU: *How old is he?*

ME: I'm not sure—late forties I think. Anyway, the problem is that he doesn't listen or seem to relate to me.

YOU: *Have you tried discussing it with him?*

ME: Yes. Heaps of times.

YOU: *Does he have a hearing problem do you think?*

ME: No.

YOU: *How about going to a counsellor?*

Giving advice

For the purpose of listening and building relationships, giving advice is rarely appropriate. It is not helpful, because it is your solution. When you advise, you most often are serving *your* needs. Think about it—aren't you serving yourself by telling somebody what they ought, should or must do? Are you really focused on what is best for them or is it possible that you may be enjoying having the superior position, right answer or best experience? (You have very little room to move with this question—notice that it is *closed* and I have given you limited options. Do you have a strong sense that I am trying to get you to agree with me and see it my way? Quite different from the questions in the preceding section isn't it?)

Advice is an obvious form of *power-over* communication. It's I win–you lose because I have the superior knowledge.

However, giving *information* when you have some that the talker is not aware of may prove helpful. There is quite a difference between information—for example, 'We will be finishing the course tonight at 6 o'clock, not 7 o'clock'—and advice—'You would be better off going home early.'

I attended a training program once where the facilitator said that any advice 'is unasked for criticism'. I've pretty well believed that ever since. In my experience, most people who ask for your advice don't actually want it. What they are really looking for is your help in finding their own solutions. Active listening techniques and open questions go a long way towards assisting people to do this.

Think back to the number of times you have told somebody what they should do (whether they asked for this or not). What was your most common response? Many people tell me that they commonly hear 'Oh, but I can't because . . .' or 'Well, the trouble with that is . . .'

Again, I urge you to trial this yourself. On a couple of occasions tomorrow, give advice to someone and on a couple of other occasions, don't—simply ask them some open questions (perhaps involving what they see as their options or opportunities).

Step 3 of listening

Active listening techniques and open questions alone are not enough for excellent listening. Whilst they can go a long way towards responding to someone, after some time of talking most of us need some more proof that we are truly being understood. The best proof is some kind of summary of what has been heard. This response is a 'paraphrase'.

If after I had told you my story about my relationship with my brother (see pages 90–2) and you used any of the following responses, I would feel that I had been well and truly heard:

'*I sense* you're unhappy about your brother's responses to you.'

'*Sounds like you* have tried a number of things and none of them has been the solution.'

'*So what you are saying is* that your relationship with your brother is not at all to your liking.'

'*You are* wondering what to do next and you think you have a new solution.'

Each of the paraphrases above summarises what I was saying at some stage during my conversation. A summary such as any of these is a positive and powerful force in building a relationship of trust between two people because the responses indicate to the person telling the story that the message has been understood and accepted.

Levels of paraphrase

There are three levels at which you can paraphrase a person. Firstly there is *parroting*, which is where you repeat to the person almost exactly what they said to you. For example, if I said to you 'I love my weekends. They are when I finally get to do what I really love to do' and you paraphrase me by saying 'Sounds like you really love your weekends as they are when you get to do what you really love to do', you will have really only used a parrot of my words. This is quite annoying for the talker and grates for all parties concerned. Parroting in many respects is simply a poor paraphrase, and often occurs because the person isn't practised at this listening skill.

A better response is a true *paraphrase*. A paraphrase is a summary of what you heard the person say—the content or the story that they said. It is often shorter than their own version and it conveys the basic essence or gist of the message as opposed to all of the words and details. For example, 'I sense your weekends are important to you' is a paraphrase. 'So you look forward to weekends' is a paraphrase.

Paraphrase is also *non-judgmental*—it should not include your opinion or judgment of the 'rightness' or 'goodness' of the talker's comment. Judgmental listening is power-over relating. Restating without any of *your* views is power-with communication.

As you improve at paraphrasing and it becomes a more natural habit (this takes no longer than a week or two for many of us), you might like to leave off the usual beginnings of paraphrases such as 'Sounds like . . .', 'I sense . . .' or 'What you're saying is . . .' and begin your paraphrases with the word 'You're . . .'—'You're looking forward to the weekend.' Be careful not to start this habit too early because 'You're . . .' closely resembles a 'you statement'. Remember that 'you statements' often lead immediately into a diagnosis, a label or an interpretation as opposed to an accurate restatement of what was said.

The next level of paraphrase is often called a *reflection*. A reflection is where you paraphrase the *feelings* that you thought were implied in the person's message. This is not always possible because people do not always indicate any emotion; however, someone banging a clenched fist on a table while they are speaking could be reflected by a 'You are angry about this situation' or 'I sense you are very angry about what people have been doing on this project and the lack of progress to date.'

EXERCISES

Exercise 1 for tonight
At some time this evening, paraphrase somebody once or twice. If you feel useless, like you are not doing anything when you paraphrase, don't be fooled. Notice the positive effect and warm feelings being generated in the talker. Your paraphrase offers the talker a service. It says 'You can go ahead, I am really listening'.

For example, if somebody you live with comes home this evening and says 'I had a terrible day', you could answer by way of an assertion—'So did I, I had a lot of trouble with X and I found Y difficult and . . .' Another option is to use an open question such as 'What happened?' (Can you sense the difference in the relationship dynamics if you use this?) The option I'm suggesting as a 'homework' assignment is for you to *paraphrase* the person. Say something like 'You seem unhappy with the day' or 'I sense you are feeling pretty down about it'.

To paraphrase somebody this evening, take a few moments to process what you have heard and then rephrase to check that you have understood them.

Exercise 2

For many people, it is easier to learn the skill of paraphrasing by starting out writing some paraphrase responses and then moving on to saying responses out aloud. This exercise will allow you to take some time to think about what a paraphrase of the person's comment will look and sound like.

Assume that someone has just made each of the following statements to you. Write your response to the statement as though you were speaking to the person to be sure that you have understood what they have said.

1 'I feel great today. I managed to do something just right at work.'

    _____

    _____

    _____

2 'I'm sick of trying. Every proposal I touch gets knocked back—what's the use.'

    _____

    _____

    _____

3 'My wife is a kind, thoughtful person, but she doesn't seem to understand that I like to have some time to myself, alone.'

_____

_____

_____

4 'My life is boring. I do the same thing every day.
   What bothers me is I don't seem to be able to change
   it. I'd give anything to get out of this situation.'

   _____

   _____

   _____

5 'I don't know what to do. If I go away for the
   weekend, I'll miss the dinner. If I go to the dinner,
   I'll miss the weekend. What do you think I should
   do?'

   _____

   _____

   _____

Common problems with paraphrasing

Below are some of the inappropriate habits that many
of us use when attempting to paraphrase another
person's comments. For each of the examples of inaccurate paraphrases, see if you can work out for yourself
what consequences the poor paraphrase will have on the
talker. Then read on to check my impressions of why
that paraphrase was not as useful as it could be.

ME: I feel great today. I managed to do something
      just right at work.
YOU: I sense you feel good because you finally did
      something correctly.

This paraphrase has gone too far in interpreting what

the person has said. The words 'you finally did something correctly' are quite a few steps further on from 'doing something just right at work'. When you paraphrase, be careful not to underplay or exaggerate what the person has said to you.

ME: I'm sick of trying. Every proposal I touch gets knocked back—what's the use.

YOU: That's no good. Sounds like you're feeling down about all the knockbacks you are getting at the moment.

The problem with this is in the first sentence. Remember that paraphrase is *non-judgmental* listening. It is about summing up what people have said to you. It does not include your opinion or judgments of any kind. Whilst the comment 'that's no good' may be intended as a bit of cheer or sympathy, it is bringing the listener's point of view or comments into the relationship. This takes the control away from the talker. Leave out your view and simply use the second sentence.

ME: My wife is a kind, thoughtful person, but she doesn't seem to understand that I like to have some time to myself, alone.

YOU: So, you really want to take a holiday by yourself.

This person has been overly diagnostic. This response is an analytical one. What the person has said has been extrapolated into something else. The opinion of 'needing to take a holiday' says more about the listener's way of thinking than it does about what the talker is saying. People will get very defensive if you analyse them and if your paraphrase indicates that you are diagnosing or labelling them.

ME: My life is boring. I do the same thing every day. What bothers me is I don't seem to be able to change it. I'd give anything to get out of this situation.

YOU: Seems like you feel you are in a rut.

This is an excellent paraphrase. The word 'rut' is a great synonym for what the person is saying and makes the paraphrase short which therefore does not take power away from the talker.

ME: I don't know what to do. If I go away for the weekend, I'll miss the dinner. If I go to the dinner, I'll miss the weekend. What do you think I should do?

YOU: Sounds like you have a dilemma and need to sit down and work it out carefully.

The first part is fine: 'sounds like you have a dilemma' is an accurate summary of what the person has said. The next part is advice. Many people fall into the trap of using paraphrase as a sneaky way of telling people what they really ought to do. Remember advice is 'unasked for criticism'.

If you are still unsure about my contention that *telling people what to do* is inappropriate, imagine yourself in this scenario: Somebody has told you they are in a dilemma about whether to go to dinner or away for the weekend. You tell them that they should 'go for the weekend because it is longer'. What's the most likely response from somebody who has been given that advice?

Most people tell me that the other person will say something like 'Oh, but then I will miss the dinner'. If you then say 'Well, in that case go to the dinner', the answer is very likely to be 'Oh, but then I will miss the weekend'.

The person talking needs your help in their own solving of the problem, *not* your advice.

Exercise 3
For each of the statements being made, imagine that someone has just said this to you and respond *out aloud*. Do not write your answer to these, say them after a few moments to process what you have heard.

> 'I need a holiday, I think. Everything is getting on top of me. Just to get away from it all, you know?'

> 'I love being with my children. They are great kids!'

> 'I get a great deal of pleasure from doing up my old home.'

> 'I don't like people who give other people a hard time. My office is full of this sort of thing at the moment. People just don't seem to be able to help themselves.'

> 'I don't know . . . it's just that . . . well . . . I don't know.'

Did you find that it is becoming easier to sum up what the person has said? Remember that people enjoy being listened to and they really like to be paraphrased.

Some of us tend not to paraphrase fairly short comments such as the sentences above. Many of us prefer to sum up only the longer conversations. Have a go now at verbally paraphrasing these comments.

> 'I don't like going to the beach. I much prefer the

mountains. I always find the beach too crowded, I don't like the heat, the sand annoys me and I find everything too expensive. I'm a cold climate person really, I like the cool of the mountains, I love going for walks, I always feel like I'm on a real holiday if I go inland.'

Now paraphrase and/or reflect back the gist of what you have heard from this person.

What you have just demonstrated is called a 'focus'. Focusing is simply a large or 'longer paraphrase' and is very useful for summing up people who have a number of points they are making to you. Another great use for a focus is a person who has a habit of repeating themselves or giving you very wordy explanations of what they are thinking or feeling. Focuses quite often start like this:

'So, let me see if I have understood you correctly so far . . .'
or
'Let me see if I'm following you correctly. You feel . . .'

Try another focus in response to this comment:

'I'm sick and tired of all of this. I am not going to put up with it any more. You have been rude to me on a number of occasions now and no matter what I tell you you just keep on doing it. You are not open to any feedback that is negative and as soon as I tell you when I'm not happy you accuse me of criticising you. You are a rude and ignorant person and I refuse to tolerate your bad behaviour any longer.'

You may not feel like paraphrasing this person and you may feel more inclined to assert yourself in terms of some 'I statements' on your views of the matter. You are learning to paraphrase and focus at the moment, and being able to use a paraphrase to settle a person down by showing them that you have heard their point of view *before* you begin to disagree with them and explain your point of view is a very powerful tool for problem solving. The next chapter covers this in more detail.

Exercise 4
Paraphrase has a number of uses. Use paraphrase for the next few examples even though they are comments that would most commonly not elicit such a response from most people.

> 'That wasn't a bad effort the other day. Didn't know you had it in you.'

A paraphrase such as 'I sense you're surprised at my achievement the other day' puts the pressure back on the person making the sarcastic comment. It asks them to straighten themselves up—to say yes or no to what position they are really taking up. Paraphrase is useful for this purpose.

> 'What the hell are you talking about? Doesn't make any sense!'

If you paraphrase with 'It sounds like you're not sure what I'm on about' you are diffusing a potentially volatile and aggressive situation. By calmly paraphrasing somebody's point of view, you are sending a signal that you are not about to be inflamed by their comments and that you are interested in sorting the situation out.

> 'Back off Fred!'

If you paraphrase with 'I sense you really want me to leave this alone' you are actually using the first step of the advanced technique of handling resistance. You are not reacting aggressively or even trying to put your point of view to a person who is not yet ready to listen. Instead, you are using a technique of showing the person that you are comprehending their point of view. As you will learn in the next chapter, this is a very useful first step in negotiating with somebody who is in conflict with you.

Exercise 5

Many people who need to counsel employees or others like to be able to reflect feelings when they paraphrase. Often an accurate reflection of a person's feelings cuts right through to the 'heart of the matter' and enables a more honest and direct conversation to take place.

If you want to be able to reflect people's feelings do the following exercises:

PURPOSE:	To learn active listening responses that accurately *reflect* the other person's thoughts and feelings.
DIRECTIONS:	In each of the following situations, the other person is letting you know that s/he is experiencing a problem. 1 Write the feeling you think the other is expressing, then 2 Write a response that reflects feelings of the other person as you heard them.
EXAMPLE:	'Well, don't you think you would have done the same thing if you were in my shoes? Wouldn't everyone feel that way?' *Feelings*: Worried, concerned. *Reflection*: 'I sense that you're worried about whether you handled it okay.'

Person at work says:

1 'I wish my boss would let me know more often how I'm doing. She never tells me what she thinks about my work.'
   Feelings:
   Reflection:

2 'All right, I said I was sorry didn't I? What more do you want me to do? I know I was wrong.'
   Feelings:
   Reflection:

3 'I don't care what happens any more. Why bother? It's pointless trying to improve anything here.'
   Feelings:
   Reflection:

Step 4 of listening

The fourth step of listening to a person is to use some of the *open questions* I discussed in Step 2 that were specifically about leading people towards their own solutions to their problems.

After you have actively listened to a person (asked them a couple of open questions to encourage them to talk further and summed up what they are saying from time to time, either in terms of the story they are telling or the feelings they are implying), it becomes particularly appropriate to ask them what they think *they can do* about the situation.

Questions such as 'What are your options do you think?' or 'What's the solution do you think?' often elicit an immediate set of possibilities from the talker.

Some people are not ready to deal with solutions or

genuinely can't think of any, so the final stage of listening may involve you doing either:

- some more paraphrasing to sum up where they are at present or
- asking some questions about what they have tried and what the consequences of those actions were or
- asking *again* what are some of the possible solutions now or in the future.

A process design to follow for counselling

Figure 3.2 is not just the stages of really listening to another person, it also provides a very helpful model for *how to counsel* somebody. This type of process would be seen as a fairly *humanistic* approach because it assumes that people can find the solutions to their own problems if they are cared for, listened to attentively and treated empathically. While it is probably true that there are

Figure 3.2: Summary of steps in attending/responding

Summary of steps in attending/responding	
Step 1 Active listening Mental alertness Eye contact Nodding and 'uh-huh's Mirroring	*Step 3 Paraphrase/reflecting/focus* 'So . . .' 'What you're saying is . . .' 'I sense . . .' 'Sounds like you are . . .'
Step 2 Open questions 'Tell me more . . .' 'Go on . . .' 'How do you feel about that?' 'I'm not sure I understand . . .'	*Step 4 Ask for solutions (problem solving)* 'What do you think you can do?' 'What have you tried?' 'What will you try?' 'What are your options?'

some people who fall outside of this assumption, for most people in a work or home situation these steps are immensely useful when we are trying to sort out an issue, a problem or in simply getting heard.

There are numerous other techniques that can be put into a counselling session and most books on the subject of counselling and 'skilled helping' will explain these.

I am often asked if when you are listening it is 'okay' to share some of your own similar experiences that may prove 'helpful' for the listener. While I can see that it may help people feel less alone to know that someone else has had a similar sort of problem, I also believe that helping people and listening to people is probably best achieved by not letting you get in their way. Trial it. Pay attention to the *response* of the talker and then make up your own mind.

Performance review

For those of you who are involved in employee perfor-mance appraisal and counselling, the stages of listening are very relevant to this process. Because of the nature of the procedure that you need to follow, you may at times need to have *input* by way of your own *opinion* and *feedback* on the staff member's performance. This can easily fit in to the process design of Figure 3.2.

A useful rule of thumb for many managers is to allow the employee to talk first, explaining their point of view and offering solutions of their own *before* you give them your views and time frames. Remember, your views need to be *assertive* : 'I need . . .', 'I want . . .'. It is always easier to influence a staff member towards changed behaviour if they have been heard and understood *before* you assert what your needs and requirements are. Chapter 4 deals with issues of influencing people in more detail.

Back to issues of power

Listening to people empowers them. Sharing of power is the basis of the culture shift away from *power-over* towards *power-with* others. If you can afford to use these listening habits you will not only enhance your own relationships, you may be part of a critical mass of people beginning to change our culture.

4
Advanced
Interpersonal
Skills

WHO NEEDS TO DO ADVANCED SKILLS?

Advanced interpersonal skills are the basic or prerequisite skills of Chapters 2 and 3 strategically combined. They are not new skills, rather ways of applying the skills covered in Chapters 2 and 3—assertive talking and listening.

When we need to *deal with resistance* and have roles or responsibilities that involve leading or *influencing* others, it is important to be able to use interpersonal skills effectively in conflict situations. It is potentially difficult to negotiate a win–win solution using a collaborative problem-solving approach without being able to use the 'power-with' interpersonal skills that may make or break the entire effort.

If, in your work, you consult, manage, make decisions or negotiate, then you need *advanced* interpersonal skills.

Consider Figure 4.1 and notice that the strategy involves listening and responding to an irate person *before* arguing back with your own assertions.

Figure 4.1: Handling conflict

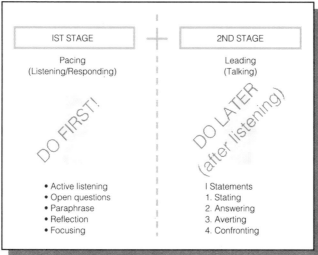

Some people mismanage conflict because they are either aggressive or passive. They immediately try to beat somebody or they allow somebody to beat them. Others, who can speak assertively, rush to argue with somebody who is resisting them, not realising the positive outcomes that are possible by strategically adjusting the order of how to deal with this seemingly 'difficult' personality.

In a nutshell, successfully dealing with conflict involves using assertion skills in the order of *listening first* and *then asserting* your needs once the person has settled down somewhat. It's called 'pacing' and 'leading'. This is *power-with* communication at its most 'powerful'.

Figure 4.2: Advanced formula for handling resistance and influencing

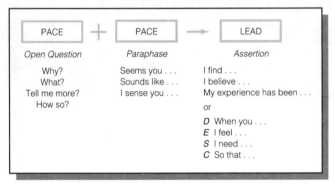

PACE	+	PACE	→	LEAD
Open Question		*Paraphase*		*Assertion*
Why?		Seems you . . .		I find . . .
What?		Sounds like . . .		I believe . . .
Tell me more?		I sense you . . .		My experience has been . . .
How so?				or
				D When you . . .
				E I feel . . .
				S I need . . .
				C So that . . .

PACING AND LEADING TO HANDLE RESISTANCE

You will notice that pacing involves taking time to hear the person's point of view and summing this up before making your own 'I statement'. The way to influence people to hear your point of view is to join them where they are at first and then lead them wherever you would like them to follow.

This is not manipulating another person. Pacing uses win–win, collaborative and problem-solving interpersonal dynamics to achieve a satisfactory result for both parties. Pacing is a fairly natural occurrence whereby two opposites are brought together because one person is prepared to join the other to gain more understanding, and then asks the other person to do the same for them.

As a counsellor, I know that in order to influence a client to consider another way of viewing things, the client has to be attended to in a deep and powerful way *before* they will allow me to lead them into considering other possibilities. Neurolinguistic programming is one form of therapy that advocates *mirroring* the person (see Chapter 3 for details) then *pacing*, then *leading*. This sets up a fairly natural rhythm of mirror, pace, lead . . . mirror, pace, lead . . .

For the purpose of this chapter's attention on advanced interpersonal skills for handling resistance and overcoming conflict, the rhythm is going to be pace, pace, lead . . . pace, pace, lead . . . and so on.

HANDLING A 'DIFFICULT' PERSONALITY

The best way to demonstrate the use of pacing and leading is in a situation where you are asserting your opinion and you encounter *resistance*. This can come in many forms, ranging from vaguely 'stroppy' to openly attacking. Imagine you are in conversation with another person and you are assertively stating your opinion on which season of the year you prefer.

You might say, 'Isn't it wonderful that summer is over. I hate summer, it's too hot. I love winter and pretty soon we will be into some cool weather.' Imagine that the person you have been talking to cuts you off before you have finished and, with exasperation in their face and tone of voice, says to you: 'What! Don't be ridiculous. What's the matter with you? Summer is the best season by far.'

You have just encountered resistance in the form of a person who seems angry and tense and appears to have a completely opposing opinion. What are your options here? Consider the way you would normally deal with someone who resists you in this way. Do you tend to get into passive patterns, aggressive retorts, or are you one of the few people who are skilled at handling this potential 'drama' assertively?

Being passive

If you are a *passive* person, or tend to use passive habits when you are under pressure in conflict situations, you are likely at this point to back down in some shape or form. A passive response would be: 'Oh well, yeah, I suppose . . .' Some passive people try using a closed question in this situation to see if they can manipulate the person into changing their mind or being more 'moderate'. An example of this would be: 'But don't you think that summer can get a little too humid for some people?' or 'But wouldn't you agree that winter has some good points?' A likely answer from the resister would involve some form of saying no and even some escalation in their irritation. The problem of dealing with resistance has not been resolved nor have both people had their viewpoints heard or understood. Passive techniques are not going to collaboratively solve this problem.

What many passive people do, once they don't score any 'wins' for themselves using this approach, is use some form of payback at a later date. The passive person who has not had their point of view heard or accepted in this instance may later seek revenge. When asked for assistance by the other person they may retort: 'I'm sorry I can't help you. I'm too busy.' This is a payback for not listening to them or treating them harshly earlier.

Passive people sometimes like to talk about people with whom they are having difficulty behind their backs; for example, saying to a colleague: 'Don't you find Mary irritating, the way she always insists on harping about the heat. She is also quite slow at her work, I've been told.'

Being aggressive

Aggressive people, or people who have a tendency to fall into aggressive patterns when they are dealing with conflict, tend to argue immediately, attempting to 'beat' the other person by 'winning' the argument. Replies such as: 'Rubbish! Winter is lovely and cool and summer is hopeless' or 'Well, of course, most of the research indicates that the majority of people prefer winter and that is why many of our overseas visitors choose winter for vacations here.' (Notice the aggressive use of 'power-over' tactics by mentioning research and the majority of people, 'everyone' and the like.)

The likely response from the resister is usually a more determined position and often escalated aggression such as: 'Well I know lots of people who prefer summer. In fact, most of my friends prefer it because you can go to the beach and enjoy outdoor activities. I couldn't give a damn about your research.'

Aggression is not going to solve the problem of either dealing with the resister's irritation or having both parties' points of view heard.

Speaking assertively

An assertive person might answer back: 'Well, I prefer winter. It's my preference because I like the cold and I very much enjoy sitting by the fire in the evenings.' The resister is likely to reply with more of their viewpoint and with the same level of irritation; for example, 'Who likes the cold? Not all of us can sit by fireplaces. Some of us can't afford them. I can't understand your attitude—there must be something wrong with you.' Continuing the use of 'I statements' at this point is largely wasted because the person resisting, being too caught up in their own irritation, is not able to hear. *Speaking* assertively is not enough during conflict—you need to *listen* assertively to solve the problem.

I recommend using *pacing* and *leading* at this point, because it is a more advanced form of assertion. Take a few moments to listen to the person's point of view and draw out their argument further *before* reasserting your original point of view.

PACING AND LEADING IN ACTION

The same interaction looks and sounds different if the skills of listening before asserting are employed. Let's say that I am the person who likes winter and I am pleased that summer is finished. I am talking to Mary, who resists me both in her manner and her story.

ME: Isn't it wonderful that summer is over. I hate summer. It's too hot. I love winter and pretty soon we will be into some cooler weather.

MARY: (The resister) What! Don't be ridiculous. What's the matter with you? Summer is the best season by far.

(This is resistance both in the details of the story as well as the manner or attitude of the person. It is pointless to keep reasserting your point of view. At this point, it would be more

116

strategic to take time to understand what is
bothering Mary and what is her position.)

ME: What's your view then? (Or 'Why do you say
that?' or 'I'm not sure I understand what you
mean.')

(Notice that I am using *open questions* to draw
out the person but I could also use a *paraphrase*;
for example, 'I sense you have a completely
different view from mine' or 'You disagree
strongly with my preference for winter.' A *paraphrase or an open question is how you pace
somebody*.)

MARY: Everyone knows that summer is a more pleasant
season than winter, which is just too cold and
miserable. Summer is better because you have
longer days to go to the beach and play sport.
It's a much more active time.

(While Mary has probably appreciated some 'air
time' to express her point of view in detail, she
is unlikely to have settled down enough after
just one 'pace' to be ready to listen to my
reassertion. At this point, it is probably more
helpful if I pace her again and, if necessary
again, until I sense she has settled enough to
hear my reassertion.)

ME: So, you much prefer summer because of the
things you are able to do in that season.

(Notice this is a *paraphrase*, however, I could
have used an *open question*. In pacing, open
questions and paraphrasing are completely inter-
changeable. Open questions are best used to
draw out someone who is not speaking much or

is being sullen. Paraphrasing often is more suitable for someone who has had a lot to say and
needs proof that they have actually been heard.)

MARY: Yes, that's right.

(You will often hear a person who has been
paced say words like 'that's right' or 'exactly'.
This is because if a person has been listened to,
encouraged to have their say and summed up
accurately, they have little need to go on resisting you.

We will stop the dialogue at this point to draw out what
has been happening in terms of the pacing and leading
model. At this stage, only the *pacing* has been completed. We haven't yet achieved a real win–win,
collaborative effort because Mary has had most of the
air space and only her point of view has been heard.
This will be rectified shortly by use of the *leading* part
of the equation.

Figure 4.3 shows where I have travelled so far in this
encounter. I began by asserting my opinion on a preference for winter but I ran into a 'brick wall' in the

Figure 4.3: Handling resistance

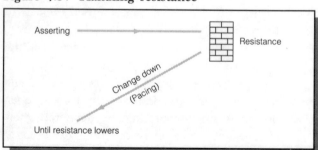

form of resistance. To encounter the resistance I have changed down a gear in preparation for negotiating the steeper gradient. The point where I am now, with Mary saying 'yes, that's right', is where I believe her resistance has lowered. She need not agree with me, nor move from her point of view, but her tone of voice and her general demeanour are likely to indicate to me that she has less resistance, anger or need to speak than she previously had. A reassertion now needs to be brought into play, as shown in Figure 4.4.

Once the resistance has settled down a little, it is time to re-establish my perspective and point of view by using 'I statements'.

Now back to the dialogue. I had just finished para-phrasing Mary.

ME: So, you much prefer summer because of the things you are able to do in that season.

MARY: Yes, that's right.

ME: Well, I disagree. I prefer winter and always have. I like the cold climate and I feel more active at that time of the year.

Figure 4.4: Handling resistance before reasserting

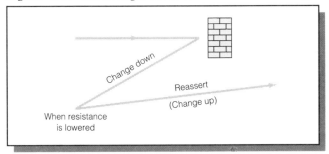

(My reassertion needs to use 'I statements'. It would be inappropriate for me to launch into broad, sweeping 'you statements' such as 'Well, you must realise that many of *us* prefer winter and you should try to see it in a more positive light . . .')

By the end of this process of pacing and leading, what has occurred is that both parties have had their say and been heard. The resistant person has been settled by the pacing technique to enable them to hear what I want to say. Quite often, the person is *influenced* towards an appreciation of the other person's point of view when they did not intend to give it any time or credence. Sometimes the resister will make a final comment such as: 'Well you are entitled to your point of view' or 'Yes, well, winter has some good features.' In this way, the person is influenced to move from their own position of strong resistance to genuine acceptance of another viewpoint.

Some managers ask me why I think this process has achieved anything. They say things such as: 'But nobody has the right answer or agreed to a final solution'. Bear in mind that this is not about one person *winning* and the other person *losing*. There may not be a simple or perfect 'answer'. The aim is to ensure different viewpoints are able to coexist with each other. The outcome is shared power due to *power-with* problem solving.

Further resistance

By the way, Mary may not have finished her argument here. She may choose to re-resist after my final re-assertion. She may come back with a comment such as: 'In actual fact, I think that spring is the best season and that seems to be the opinion of most Australians.' At this point I would need to attend to her continued resistance by using some more *pacing*. I can choose the form of open questions or paraphrasing to show my listening before I reassert my view.

ME: I sense you feel strongly that winter is not a good season. (Paraphrase the continued resistance.)

MARY: Yes I do actually.

ME: It's my favourite time of year. (Reassert.)

Forms of resistance

Sometimes, you can tell resistance because you can hear or see anger, resentment or unacceptance. Often the person's resistance is obvious because they have a great deal to say in opposition to you on the topic. You may see non-verbals that are indicating to you the person is tense, excited or irritated by what you have said. It may be the topic or you that is bothering the person. They could be angry or upset about something else but will attempt to take it out on you.

In other instances, the resistance is camouflaged. Indirect forms of resistance include the following habits:

- *Excusing*—some people have a habit of telling you why they couldn't do something or how they were going to do something, however, when used as a pattern of relating to you this is a form of resistance.
- *Sabotaging*—occurs when some of your needs, time or even material possessions are damaged or mis-

treated. Children are good at sabotaging your best-laid plans by putting on a tantrum or banging a drum while you are trying to sleep. Adults also are very good at sabotaging your requirements by transgressing the boundaries of what you see as your rights.

- *Ignoring*—this is where your point of view is fairly consistently ignored. You find the other person's behaviour pays no attention to what you have clearly stated you need or can't tolerate.

- *Ridiculing*—happens when someone you live or work with has a habit of mocking you or joking about you in a way that indicates they are not taking you seriously.

- *Paying people back*—includes sulking behaviour, the silent treatment and a variety of other forms that are someone's attempt to make you sorry for something that you have said or done earlier.

- *Making mistakes*—involves someone who has a habit of getting things wrong, mucking things up and seems never able to deliver 100 per cent of what was required.

- *Arguing*—involves a person who always seems to have to argue and debate with you on what seems to be a fairly small matter. It seems like there are major discussions or argument on any point of choice.

- *Fighting*—happens by physical push, shove or worse. The sad reality of our society is that many people are assaulted and abused daily by members of their own family.

Before you begin pacing and leading techniques to deal with these other forms of resistance, consider the causes of these behaviours. In my opinion most people do not get out of bed in the morning and prepare a 'hit list' of whose day they are going to 'destroy'. Most people indulge in these resistant behaviours because they feel that they are not surviving equally in the relationship. If you know someone who uses excusing or the silent treatment with you, ask yourself what you are doing that may be causing them to feel that they do not have enough power in the relationship.

Many of us fall into these habits we have been socialised into, particularly by our family. It is not unusual to see couples attempting to relate to each other by combining forms of resistance and counter-resistance. This is dysfunctional, causes a lot of pain to each person, and uses huge amounts of energy that could be otherwise channelled into moving forward towards common goals.

The various forms of resistance are simply *power-over* patterns we have picked up from our role models.

If you are living with somebody who has a habit of always forgetting to wipe the benchtops after washing up or forgetting how to use the dryer and they always have a good excuse for why this is so, ask yourself how are you relating to them. For example, did you bounce out of bed on Sunday morning and tell your partner 'Right, let's get cracking! Go in the kitchen and finish last night's washing up and then I want you to mow the back lawn while I weed the vegetable patch and then I'll put some lunch together. That way we can go to the movies this afternoon.'

It may be that your partner finds you too bossy or

your style of speaking may be aggressive as opposed to assertive. If this is the case, you are likely to find that forms of resistance such as forgetting the benchtops will become their unconscious or conscious habit of regaining some power.

People who persist in patterns of passive resistance after becoming aware of it need to take responsibility for the consequences of their actions. The skills of pacing and leading are extremely useful to assist your negotiations with someone by drawing out their point of view, hearing it (and giving the person some respect by doing so), then asserting your needs and requirements and insisting on being heard yourself. From now on, it becomes necessary to negotiate on the basis of 'what are *your whats*' (refer back to page 39), 'what are *my whats*', and do we have some that overlap? Do we need to go in different directions to satisfy our needs or how might we compromise to solve the problem?

An exercise

At this point, I would like you to stop thinking about these concepts in theory and have a go at some practical basic pacing and leading.

For each of the scenarios below you will need to imagine that someone has just spoken to you and is resisting you. You need to pace them by way of a *paraphrase* and wait for their response. Then, with their resistance lowered you would go ahead and assert your opinion.

1 'I can't do it for you. I'm too busy Who has the time to organise meetings with people from all over the

place?' (You need the person to set up a meeting for you.)
Paraphrase:

_____

_____

_____

Imagine that the person's resistance has lowered after your paraphrase.
Assert:

_____

_____

_____

2 'You know how to put food on a plate as well as I do. I'm not going anywhere near the kitchen for a while. I'm reading.' (You have asked your partner would they put together some lunch for both of you because you are in the middle of writing an assignment and don't want to lose your momentum.)
Paraphrase:

_____

_____

_____

Imagine that the resistance has lessened enough for you to assert your needs.
Assert:

_____

_____

_____

3 'Okay, I'll do it. Don't expect much, though. Not

with this little notice.' (You want the job done thoroughly and well.)

Paraphrase:

_____

_____

_____

Assert:

_____

_____

_____

4 'Dinner! How can I go to dinner? There are a hundred things I have to get done. I'm so far behind.' (You want to go to dinner with your partner.)

Paraphrase:

_____

_____

_____

Assert:

_____

_____

_____

How did you go? Of course, it may take more than one paraphrase to settle a person enough for them to be able to hear your needs or concerns. The exercise is to give you practice in learning to listen before you speak assertively.

Dealing with legitimate power

I have been asked many times how pacing and leading can be used in situations with a person who has more legitimate power in the 'system' than you. An example of this would be your boss in a usual work environment. Bosses have more 'rank' and can use their position in the hierarchy to have 'power-over' others. Pacing and leading is enormously useful in this situation. I use these skills almost daily with clients. Pacing and leading is a handy tool when you are consulting with people who feel they are ultimately more powerful than you, that is, because they are paying your fee.

In Figure 4.5 the left-hand column of beliefs and behaviours represents the traditional manager who operates from a position of wanting to keep all the power. As mentioned in Chapter 1, there is a significant cultural swing in our society and our workplaces towards the right-hand column of values which are about co-operative, collaborative problem solving. Assertion, including pacing and leading techniques, is entirely consistent with this vision of leaders who can afford to give power to staff by asking questions, listening, being able to sum up, and when stating their own opinion, using 'I statements' rather than power-over 'you statements'.

Figure 4.5: Styles of leadership power

LEGITIMATE POWER	RELATIONSHIP POWER
Power of rank	Power of interpersonal skills
Power-over	Power-with
Win	Win ⟷ Win
↕	
Lose	
'I keep the power'	'I give you power'

If we apply this concept to you as a leader or supervisor of someone else, it requires *you* to use these skills when you are encountering resistance in the person who is legitimately more 'junior' to you. In other words, it is not acceptable to tell a staff member to 'just do it'. It is preferable for you to listen to their point of view and sum them up before you reassert what your requirements are.

When you are the supervisor

Let's assume that you are talking with an employee about a deadline which you have set for Wednesday and s/he wants it changed to Friday. Pacing and leading would take the course of you asking them why they held this opinion, listening (nodding, 'uh-huh' and so on) and summing them up. You would then decide on what you needed to assert (whether your opinion was changed by what you had heard or whether you wanted to reassert your original contention). The pacing and leading may go something like this:

YOU: I absolutely need this to be done by Wednesday at 5 o'clock.

STAFF: You're kidding! It's impossible, Friday is more like it.

YOU: (Pacing to handle the resistance) What's the problem?

STAFF: We are two people short this week due to illness and if you insist on a Wednesday deadline the quality of the work will be affected. I can't understand why people can't realise what is involved in this work and just how much time and effort we have to put in to get the job done right.

YOU: You are concerned that I understand what it is going to take to do the job well and you believe that Wednesday is too short a deadline to do this, particularly with people away sick.

STAFF: That's right.

YOU: (Leading—and deciding not to change your original position) I do need this done by 5 o'clock on Wednesday at the very latest. Also, I can't afford for it to be in any way second rate in quality. There are a whole host of factors contributing to my decision and even though I understand and accept your point of view on this occasion, I can't adjust the time frame.

(You may, after listening to the employee's perspective, change your mind and prefer to assert something like this) I take your point. However, Friday is completely out of the question considering that I have to present to the board on Thursday. The best I can do is say we can extend the deadline until Thursday lunchtime.

Pacing and leading has enabled both parties to be heard and even though your opinion may not have changed, the employee has been respected, listened to and understood. From this position it is much easier for people to accept and be led by you as the manager or supervisor.

When you are the staff member

Similarly, pacing and leading can be used by you when you are in the 'subordinate' position and the person with more legitimate power is disagreeing with you. Rather than passively accepting this unequal power dynamic or aggressively trying to beat it, use pacing to sum up your position and assert your difference in perspective. Although the other party has the final decision, and may do whatever they want anyway, this gives you the power. Imagine that *you* are the *staff member* wanting the deadline to be extended until Friday. You are dealing with your boss who may be quite traditional and absolutist in style The conversation could go like this:

BOSS: I need this job to be completed by 5 o'clock on Wednesday at the absolute latest.

YOU: I don't believe it can be done to top standard by Wednesday. We really need until Friday. We are two staff down this week.

BOSS: No, Friday is impossible. I must have it by Wednesday and that is all there is to it!

YOU: You seem concerned about this, and you want it done within the time frame that you have set. (Paraphrase)

BOSS: That's right. I'm getting pretty sick and tired of people asking for extensions and telling me sad stories about why everything is too hard. I want things done the way I ask the first time.

YOU: You seem annoyed about the reasons and excuses people give for not getting things done as asked.

BOSS: Exactly!

YOU: I am concerned about what you are saying. I believe that it is part of my responsibilities to give you feedback on when I think the time limits are going to cause problems for us in production. I don't believe this is a case of making excuses because I genuinely feel the quality of the work will be compromised. We are quite simply short-staffed.

Although your boss has the power to ignore you or remain steadfast, you are entitled to listen, sum up and reassert your position or concerns.

How not to lose

It is impossible for someone to beat you if you see winning as being allowed to have your own point of view and express it. The other person is allowed to disagree with you. That is their right. Even an aggressive boss, behaving in a totally power-over way, is still able, within most systems, to get away with this behaviour. However, you are *allowed to speak*. So state your point of view even if you know it's going to be ignored. Personal empowerment comes from knowing what your stance is and stating it out loud. Below are some win–win options that you might like to use for various situations at home or work.

Remember, these are all *leads* and need to come after appropriate *pacing*.

Agreeing to differ

'Well, it sounds like you think . . . and I think . . . It sounds like we are not going to agree on this one, so I'd be happy to leave it there. How do you feel about that?'

Negotiation

'So you'd prefer . . . and I'd rather . . . I'd like to find a solution that we are both happy with. What options can you think of?'

Compromise

'I have heard your opinion and I believe I understand your point of view which is . . . Nothing you have said, however, has changed my mind. I simply don't agree, and as you and I work (or live) together we may have a problem. How can we sort this out? Is there some position of compromise that we can arrive at?'

No room to differ

'It sounds like you really don't agree with me because . . . I just can't think of how I can meet your needs, though, because I feel . . .'

Dealing with the truly 'obnoxious'

Most people respond well to being treated in an assertive way by use of the techniques of pacing and leading. There are some people, however, who have a strong desire to 'win' and will persist in arguing with the aim of 'beating' you.

It is entirely up to you to decide for how long you wish to pace and lead someone, particularly if you sense they are being dogmatic. I tend to be prepared to pace and lead approximately three times, after which I usually decide the other party is not going to 'settle down' or co-operate in any way. Once I have listened, summed up and asserted on roughly three occasions, I tend to view the other person as attempting to force me into the losing position. This is not acceptable to me because I believe I have a right to my own opinion.

In these types of situations you might like to consider

the following styles of response. You will notice they are all *leading* responses, and should occur after the pacing (and leading) has been tried a number of times.

'I sense that you are going to persist and persist with your point of view until I agree with you. I'm not going to agree with you.'

'I don't feel like I am surviving in this conversation. I believe you are trying to win and make me lose. I reserve the right to my opinion and I am not going to continue with this style of interaction.'

Some people will continue to argue:

'But . . . you're wrong . . . your trouble is . . .'

You may need to remind them that they are continuing with the same pattern.

'You're doing more of the same right now.'

'I'm not interested in continuing this type of relationship. I'm going to leave it at that.'

'I don't wish to continue with this. I'm withdrawing my co-operation.'

Alternatively, you might like to use a DESC (from Chapter 2): 'Fred, when you keep telling me that I am wrong, I feel very frustrated and annoyed because there is no way I am going to agree with you. I need you to respect my right to my own opinion so we can agree to differ.'

You will notice that the assertions are not about the *content* (the details of the story, for example, whether Aussie Rules or League is a more enjoyable spectators' sport). The discourse is on the *process* (the way the relationship dynamics are going and the nature of the interaction). There comes a point when it is necessary to move away from *what* are we talking about to *how* are we doing this talking. Your assertion becomes one of the *relationship*, not the details.

Group dynamics

Pacing and leading is entirely consistent with the idea of *storming* (often called brainstorming or arguing) in groups or meetings. Group theory asserts that for problem solving/planning/decision making to occur, each of the stages in turn need to be successfully resolved. A group or team needs to form first (agree to the task) and then to storm. It is only once storming is resolved that norming (agreement) can take place. Similarly, it is only a normed group that is able to perform (take action) to its capacity.

In the next chapter you will see that the storming stage needs to be treated by way of high *relationship* (asking of questions, listening to other people's opinions and summarising) as well as high *task* (what to do, how to do, why and so on)(Figure 4.6). If 'relationship' is done first you have *pacing*. When 'task' is done second you have *leading*. Both 'relationship' and 'task' need to be done assertively, using the skills of listening and speaking in an assertive manner.

Chapter 5 explores the stages of group dynamics in more detail and links the interpersonal skills of Chapters 2, 3 and 4 to settings of planning, decision making and managing or leading groups of people.

Figure 4.6: The stages of group problem solving

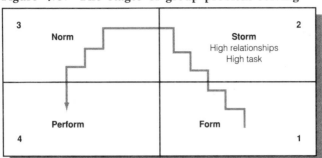

Back to issues of power

Pacing and leading is about sharing of power. The first pattern of listening non-judgmentally and then summing up to check for understanding, empowers the talker. The second step of asserting your own view without resorting to winning or losing at the other's expense, empowers you. Resistance and conflict can be dealt with, even resolved, by *power-with* communication.

5
Leadership and Teamwork

IF YOU ARE a manager or supervisor you will be interested in how these interpersonal skills relate to *leadership effectiveness* and *teamwork*. If you are involved in decision making and planning you will also be concerned with how they can be applied to *group dynamics* and the steps in *problem solving*. Similarly, people who need to attend *meetings* of any kind (including discussions with someone in conflict with you) will find this chapter useful.

The interpersonal skills outlined in Chapters 2, 3 and 4 are the same skills needed to *lead* others and manage the stages of a *relationship* with either one person or a group.

THE DIFFERENCE BETWEEN A LEADER AND A MANAGER

In industry and business circles the issue of management vs 'leadership' is current. Many managers and supervisors are told by their chief executives that they should

Figure 5.1: Changing culture

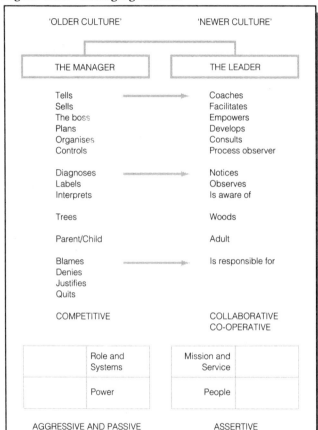

develop the skills of being a 'leader'. This shift in values attributed to good management is part of the culture change occurring in most organisations in Western countries. This is shown in Figure 5.1 below.

You will notice that the interpersonal skills linked with the more traditional style of managing staff are listed as aggressive (I win–you lose) or passive (you win–I lose). This is because conservative methods of managing have tended to include an emphasis on the legitimacy of the power wielded by the boss, because of their position of superiority in the organisational structure. Modern managers are 'leaders' if they are able to share power with staff in collaborative ways. This style of management emphasises encouragement of staff to utilise their own power (*power-within* and *power-with* others). 'Leadership' is seen as a style of managing that allows staff to exercise their own talents and choices and, as a consequence, to accept increased responsibility for themselves. Figure 5.2 represents the extremes of management power styles.

Although models are quite limited in that they reduce very complex matter into seemingly simple compartments, they can help us to conceptualise our thinking. Models of dichotomies (dividing things up into either this or that) can give the impression there are only black or white alternatives. This is not the case. We may take up one or more positions depending on circumstances. Also, there are degrees of behaviour that may fall between the two extremes. It is useful to bear in mind that people simultaneously can have various positions on a subject.

Notwithstanding these warnings regarding a limited diagnosis of managers' behaviours, this particular model has been found to be of real interest and relevance to the thousands of middle and senior managers I have led through leadership effectiveness programs.

Figure 5.2: Opposite styles of power

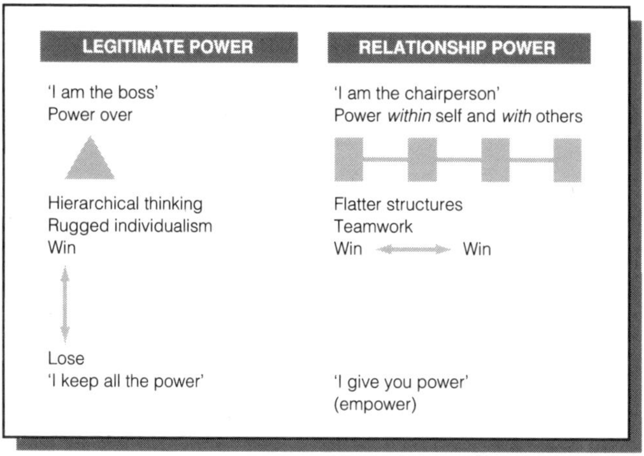

LEGITIMATE POWER	RELATIONSHIP POWER
'I am the boss'	'I am the chairperson'
Power over	Power *within* self and *with* others
Hierarchical thinking	Flatter structures
Rugged individualism	Teamwork
Win	Win ⟷ Win
Lose	
'I keep all the power'	'I give you power'
	(empower)

Notice that the 'legitimate power' style uses position over others as the main foundation of influence. Conversely, the 'relationship power' style uses relationship dynamics to lead and influence people. A comment often made by managers when considering this model is that they believe giving other people power ('I give you power') is actually a more powerful message than that given by someone who will not relinquish power and jealously guards their position.

Many of my public service clients have remarked that they find it difficult to make the shift towards shared power, as the culture in which they work historically has sent clear messages of the traditional kind. Middle managers in both the public and private sector sometimes struggle to develop a philosophy and a practice consistent with relationship power ('power-with') while realising that the behaviour of their senior managers is still embedded in the older *'power-over'* culture. The dilemma for supervisors and managers is how to change the culture from what it has been to what its mission and new structures indicate it should be, while having limited role models to encourage such efforts.

INTERPERSONAL SKILLS IN MANAGEMENT

The assertive speaking and listening skills of Chapters 2, 3 and 4 are entirely consistent with practices of sharing power. Listening to people by asking open questions, allowing them to speak and then summing them up non-judgmentally shows tolerance for the viewpoints of others. Assertive skills—owning your own statements—indicate you are aware that your opinion is only one of a number of viewpoints.

I firmly believe that managing others in a shared power arrangement is the preferred means for achieving the best outcomes and solutions for all involved. This style truly empowers all parties and sets up an environment where individuals are respected for their unique contributions. Unless a leader/manager can speak and listen assertively they will set up win–lose dynamics.

I have met many managers with excellent conceptual ability, talent in their product, and who understand the procedural tasks of management yet do not own their own statements when speaking (see Chapter 2). They therefore send an unfortunate message of 'I hold the truth on this matter', setting up win–lose power dynamics where some people are advantaged and others are disadvantaged. More effective managers/leaders are those who use their interpersonal abilities to foster the maximum utilisation of an individual's talents and needs.

Figure 5.3 shows the interpersonal skills that are most closely aligned with either legitimate (power-over) or relationship (power-with) habits of relating to others.

LEADERSHIP STYLE

A great deal has been written on the topic of 'styles of leadership', ranging from academic textbooks to self-rating personality tests which form part of a training course. Still in some use today are the models which liken laissez-faire attitudes with what is often called 'country club' management style and 'directive' patterns to a label of 'autocratic' leadership. A more complex, yet popular, model with industry managers and supervisors in industry is the Hershey and Blanchard paradigm of 'situational leadership'.

The four quadrants of situational leadership

This theory of leadership sees a leader as having a 'natural' style that they instinctively use. This habit of managing tends to fit into one or two of the following styles—*telling, selling, participating* and *delegating*. In *Management of Organisational Behaviour*, Hershey and Blanchard outline how a manager can develop skills in using the full range of leadership styles, showing how to choose the most effective quadrant for a particular staff member in a specific situation.

Figure 5.4 shows the styles in their corresponding quadrants and indicates some level of development taking place as staff increase their competency to the point where they can receive delegation. Each of the

Figure 5.3: Interpersonal styles in leadership

LEGITIMATE	RELATIONSHIP
(Power-over)	*(Power-with)*

Aggressive

You must . . .	I believe . . .
We will . . .	My preference is . . .
The team has to . . .	My position is . . .
Do X . . . Do Y . . .	I think . . .
Your problem is . . .	My problem is . . .
The fact is . . .	My view is . . .
Interrupting	Shared air space
Not asking open questions: (What is your view?)	'What's happening?' 'What's your opinion on this?' 'I'd like your view.'
Closed questions: 'Don't you think that . . .' 'Wouldn't you agree that . . .'	'Tell me your thoughts/feelings?'
'Yes but . . .'	'Yes . . . and . . .'
Labels/judgments: 'That is crazy/wrong/stupid/ not normal'	'I disagree because . . .'

Passive

Not speaking Not acting	Say what you think. Get going yourself to satisfy *your* needs.
Being rescued	Do it for yourself.
Not knowing your 'what's' (wants, beliefs)	Develop a philosophy, a vision
Blaming, denying	Taking responsibility

quadrants of leadership style has an associated blend of task and behaviour components, as Figure 5.5 indicates.

Task behaviours are defined as those that are about:

- what to do

Figure 5.4: Leadership styles

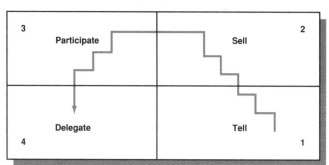

- how to do it
- when to do it by
- why it is done.

Relationship behaviours usually involve:

- asking questions
- listening
- praising
- personal conversation.

Many of us find that one or two of these styles are our preferred way of attempting to influence people. Some people even have three quadrants that they can use, indicating a greater range of leadership behaviours. Most managers I work with tend to overuse one or two quadrants at the expense of the others. It is usual to be limited to a favourite way of attempting to manage staff. There are consequences to these limitations.

For example, if you always use quadrant two (high task, high relationship) you can end up rather burned out as a manager because it is an exhausting way to

143

Figure 5.5: Task and relationship requirements for quadrants of competency

3 (Competency) High relationship Low task	(Competency) 2 High relationship High task
Low relationship Low task 4 (Competency)	High task Low relationship (Competency) 1

relate to people. You may also unknowingly create ongoing 'storming' and conflict with staff because this style of leadership encourages conflict. Additionally, many staff have competencies that are too high to warrant this style of leadership. A staff member who has good knowledge, skill and a positive attitude on a task is considerably overmanaged by this style. Similarly, a staff member whose knowledge and skill is fine but lacks confidence is not assisted by a manager using this technique.

Which management style is best?

Figure 5.5 advocates that different styles suit various staff depending on the level of *competency* of the staff member. Competency is further defined as the *knowledge*, *skill*, and *attitude* to the task of the 'follower'. This is worked out by the leader asking themselves questions: 'Does this person know how to do this in *theory*?'; 'Can they do it in *practice*?'; 'Are they *motivated* to do the task?' (keen yet not nervous). The answers to these questions tell you in which quadrant the staff member or follower is situated. The task of the leader is to use the appropriate quadrant style as it is most likely to influence the staff member and is the best use of the leader's power and talent.

A person new to the job is likely to have low knowledge, skill, and attitude, because notwithstanding their training in the area they are not yet 'competent' in applications to the specific job and leader. For many tasks, this person requires *telling* what to do. Therefore, the leader needs to be high on task and fairly low on relationship, using the Quadrant 1 style of management. (See Figure 5.6 for examples of this.)

The *manner* in which you tell people what to do is a matter of choice and your preparedness to live with the consequences of your actions. I believe that even in Quadrant 1 leadership, *assertive interpersonal style* will develop better relations with staff than aggressive or passive techniques.

The opposite to this first scenario is a person whose knowledge, skill, and attitude is high for the task at hand and therefore requires behaviour from the leader of low task and low relationship—Quadrant 4 management. The appropriate assertive examples are found in Figure 5.6.

A Quadrant 3 follower tends to have high knowledge and skill but lacks confidence for the task at hand. The style required by the leader needs to be high relationship and low task as a consequence—Quadrant 3 management.

Quadrant 2 could be said to be anything that doesn't

145

Figure 5.6: Assertive speaking and listening in situational leadership

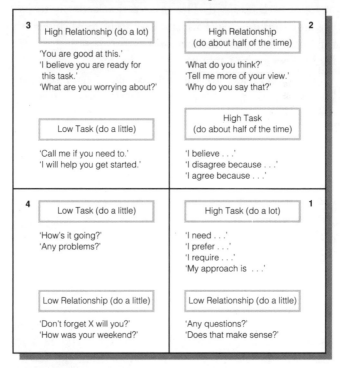

fit into the other three quadrants. More specifically, it often involves either a staff member whose knowledge and skill is high but who is bored in doing the task or someone who has only one of the three competencies. One example is someone who has enthusiasm for the task but whose knowledge and skill are not adequate for appropriate performance. In this instance, the leader needs to listen to the staff member and/or acknowledge

Figure 5.7: Leadership quadrants

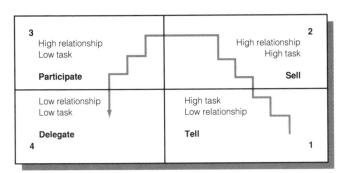

and praise them for what has been achieved (high relationship). The leader must, however, be quite detailed on what is actually required (high task).

Figure 5.7 shows the quadrants as *developmental*. Effective leadership is about developing staff competency from Quadrant 1 through to Quadrant 4 over time and as a consequence of effective management.

Regardless of which management *theories* you prefer, the *practice* of leading and managing others is greatly enhanced by your *interpersonal ability* to listen and speak *assertively*. Unless your interpersonal style is about collaboration, you may find that your habits remain largely limited to Quadrant 1 or Quadrant 2. This means that your staff can't develop high levels of competency for Quadrant 3 or Quadrant 4. Many managers unwittingly keep their staff in a less competent mode than they are capable of, by using inappropriate leadership style and/or interpersonal habits of winning and losing.

147

TEAMWORK

It is usually accepted that teamwork is a superior form of group work where the 'average' of the group members is considerably improved due to the 'synergy' of the team members. Teams are sought after in business because they tend to do better than even the best individual when they harness this synchronised energy.

Teamwork is enjoying increased popularity. This is partly due to its reputation for collaborative problem-solving (in accordance with the culture change occurring in institutions and society) and because it allows individuals to feel empowered by owning group decisions and outcomes.

Teams have been used throughout history as a more efficient and effective way of producing outcomes. Teams tend to have both *goals* (what we are doing) and *roles* (how we divide up the tasks).

In any team there are those whose personality traits lead them to take on roles that are about *vision* and there are those who are more attracted to habits within the team that are about *detail*.

The more visionary team members tend to look for creative, new ways to achieve goals. They can often see the macro context of the task as well as thinking in less orthodox ways. They often are able to resource other people's views and bring back new ideas to the team. Conversely, people whose talents lie in *detail* tend to be preoccupied with getting the task to final completion while attending to all the small details. These person-alities work in a micro context. Detail people are more into the 'trees', while vision people prefer thinking at the 'woods' level.

Good teamwork requires that both types of roles are covered. One is not better than the other. If you are highly attracted to either, however, it is easy for you to label people who are different from you as 'stupid'. It's quite common for someone concerned with completing things on time, making sure the i's are dotted and the t's are crossed, to view a visionary type as 'off with the pixies'. Similarly, people with vision can make the mistake of assuming small detail people are 'nitpickers' and 'boring'.

In addition to this axis you will notice in Figure 5.8 there is another concerning itself with *task-oriented* people and *people-oriented* people. Teamwork is more than vision and detail. It requires people who are concerned with achieving the objective as well as people who maintain team spirit and enhance the general well-being of the individuals. Task-oriented people concern themselves with getting the right results and directing the team to achieve. People-oriented members are more concerned with providing support for individuals and promoting trust and team spirit.

Figure 5.8: Teamwork roles

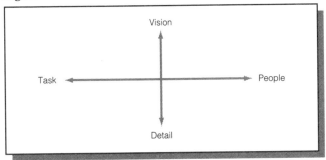

Most teams have a leader. Traditional styles of leadership have seen the task-oriented type taking on the role of shaping and driving the team. In recent times, leadership has also begun to be taken up by the personality most suited to linking all the different styles and roles of people—a chairing or facilitating role.

With a team made up of many differing types and roles, it is easy for conflict to occur. Conflict cannot be adequately resolved without good *interpersonal skills*. The ability to *listen* and *speak* in an assertive manner is critical to team functioning. The principles of collaborative problem-solving remind people in theory and in practice that while they have their opinion, other people are entitled to a different viewpoint. A task-oriented team member may push people beyond their capacities and a people-oriented member will comment on how individuals are feeling about this. The team and the individuals will be enhanced by the assertive interplay between these two styles and their points of view.

Similarly, someone concerned with perfectionism may be encouraged to stop worrying about details or to delegate more often as a consequence of communicating with a visionary team member. Understanding differences and ability to communicate from a position of interpersonal skill is critical to developing team synergy.

SOLVING PROBLEMS IN A TEAM

Teamwork is comprised of stages and each stage needs to be resolved before the next one can be attempted. In psychology the stages are known as group dynamics and are called *form*, *storm*, *norm* and *perform* (see Figure 5.9).

Figure 5.9: Stages of teamwork

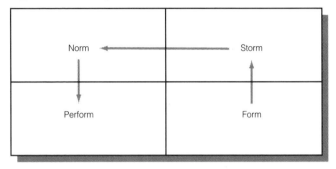

In operational terms, the considerations required for each step are as follows:

Form

- Create an atmosphere that encourages openness and sharing of information.
- Ensure that all available information about the problem is brought to light and discussed.
- State the problem in a way that everyone understands.
- Don't move on until shared understanding is reached.

Storm

- Seek ideas and opinions.
- Avoid initial judgment on evaluation of proposed solutions.
- Don't jump to your prepared solution.
- Be exhaustive in searching for solutions.
- Focus effort on the problem, not on the people.

Norm

- Narrow the range of solutions generated.
- Discuss each solution in terms of impact on you and your needs, standards and so on.
- Allow others to think through and share—the impact and implications for them.
- Critically evaluate without attacking ideas.
- Specify proposed resolution and consequences in detail.
- Agree on who is to do what, by when and with what consequences—record if necessary.

Perform

- Put plan into action (and set up a review date to monitor progress).
- Evaluate results.

These same steps are the stages that meetings need to cover in this order. For example, meetings can easily degenerate into unproductive, time-wasting exercises when time is not taken to *form* thoroughly. Without this first stage, some individuals may be thinking and speaking on issues that are sideways of the agenda.

Similarly, people cannot *storm* (brainstorm) unless they know what to talk about. Storming needs to be a healthy stage of disagreement, not a 'bun fight' characterised by people interrupting and trying to yell each other down.

People cannot *norm* (agree) in a meeting until they have been heard and had the opportunity to hear other people's viewpoints. It follows that we cannot get maximum *performance* from our team meetings until we

152

can manage these stages of teamwork and problem solving.

Figure 5.10 represents the flow chart most commonly used for business planning, decision making and teamwork. Notice how stages 1 to 4 are the same as the form, storm, norm, perform figure (Figure 5.9).

This five-box figure incorporates a final section devoted to *evaluating* whether what was achieved was actually what was set out to be achieved. The only way you can evaluate your effectiveness is against criteria that were set at the beginning. It is very hard to arrive someplace if you never set out with that destination in mind.

'Forming' is a critical part of teamwork which is often overlooked and mismanaged, as is the final stage of *evaluating* whether outcomes in line with objectives were satisfied.

THE NEED FOR INTERPERSONAL SKILLS

All these steps or stages of problem solving and teamwork could be referred to the *quality of the thinking*. While it is important that you have a logical process design such as these figures to work by, unless your interpersonal skills are effective you are unlikely to gain acceptance for your views.

It is not possible to 'form' effectively or 'brainstorm' in a functional way unless there is a relative balance between speaking assertively and listening assertively. Without these skills, the tensions in a planning or decision-making meeting can degenerate into the dysfunctional power dynamics of win–lose. For good teamwork to occur, individuals must speak and listen assertively in roughly equal proportions. Therefore, I ought to express my view approximately 50 per cent of the time and the other 50 per cent of the time I need to listen to other people's views. In some teams I may be able to perform with a 60–40 per cent or even 70–30 per cent bias, providing the bias of other team member(s) is the opposite of mine. All members of a team need to speak and listen assertively in these proportions to ensure that the quality of the thinking process is not damaged by the interpersonal domain.

Speaking assertively ensures the *task* needs of the team are satisfied. Task orientation is about getting started, sharing information, organising, giving opinion, clarifying, summarising, checking out consensus. *Listening* assertively ensures that the *people* needs of the group are covered. Examples of this are asking people questions, listening to their reasons, summing up their opinion, keeping members involved, trying to achieve harmony when there are disagreements, favourably

Figure 5.10: Business planning/decision making/ teamwork

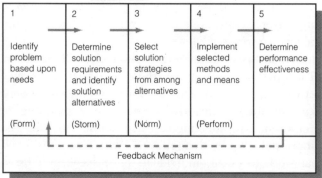

1	2	3	4	5
Identify problem based upon needs	Determine solution requirements and identify solution alternatives	Select solution strategies from among alternatives	Implement selected methods and means	Determine performance effectiveness
(Form)	(Storm)	(Norm)	(Perform)	

Feedback Mechanism

commenting on good contributions, relieving tension and so on.

In teamwork, 'self' behaviours are seen as disruptive to team outcomes because they focus on the individual winning—usually at the team's expense. Examples of behaviours that are *not assertive* or about 'task' or 'people' are: dominating the discussion, interrupting, horsing around, not listening, being aggressive, splitting hairs, smoothing over arguments, avoiding responsibility. You will notice that most of these behaviours fall into the passive or the aggressive categories of interpersonal habits.

THE LINK BETWEEN TEAMWORK AND LEADERSHIP

The stages of teamwork and group problem solving are similar to the four quadrants of leadership stages. The same process is followed by the steps or stages we go through in relationships of any kind, home or work, with an individual or a team. Figure 5.11 represents a combination of the task and relationship proportions pertaining to leading *individuals* as well as the steps and *stages* in relationships with *groups* of people.

THE HARD BIT—STORMING TO NORMING

Many managers believe that influencing an individual or a team from Stage 2 (storming) to Stage 3 (norming) is the most difficult. The critical tool for dealing with arguing is *pacing* and *leading*. Details of this are found in Chapter 4. You will remember that pacing and leading involves the use of open questions and paraphrase to listen to the argument (high relationship), and then,

Figure 5.11: The link between teamwork and leadership

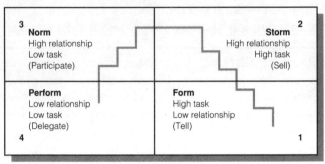

asserting and reasserting one's own point of view (high task). This communication process comprises healthy storming and is a win–win way of listening and speaking.

To move people from Quadrant 2 into Quadrant 3 needs the amount of task behaviour to be gradually lessened while maintaining high relationship behaviour (see Figure 5.11). An example of this would be to stop discussing the point of contention for a period of time while listening to the resister talk about some other topic. Alternatively, engage in some other relationship behaviour (such as personal conversation, praise, or asking questions on another topic). After a while it is important to restate your old view, but do this briefly, without causing the storming stage to be reactivated.

Imagine that you have a staff member who is in the storming stage with you in terms of your relationship progression and is therefore arguing back with you on some of your opinions. For example, they are telling you about how in their last job the procedure that they used for a task was far more efficient than 'the way things are done here'. Remember that the storming stage is healthy and natural and is simply part of the relationship being developed between you and this staff member. Remember also that the model of the quadrants is there to assist in your leadership and team development, and interpersonal skills will work in moving the person from Quadrant 2 to Quadrant 3.

The first stage is to storm 'appropriately' with the staff member. Do *relationship* first. Ask why they are saying this, or ask for details on what their former job procedures were about. Listen to what they say and sum them up non-judgmentally when they are finished; for example, 'So you think the way that you did it in your last job was faster and easier than the way we do it here'.

At this point, you have 'paced' the person. You may need to do this a couple of times depending on how 'storming' and resistant they are. When you sense they will hear you assert your view, then 'lead' the person; for example, 'Well I disagree, I believe this way works well'. You have now covered the *task* part of Quadrant 2.

Now it's time for Quadrant 3 behaviour. The next step is for you to 'back off' the task somewhat. Move to another topic or even personal conversation. For example, 'How have you been settling in here?' or 'I was very happy with your input in meetings this week.' Build a *relationship* with the staff member on another topic.

A little later in the conversation (or even the next day), make a brief *task*-related comment, such as, 'By the way, don't forget I need you to do that procedure the way I outlined. Please don't use the way you did it in your previous job.' You have now covered Quadrant 3—high relationship and low task.

If you are skeptical I recommend that you try it, because it *will* work. I've used the quadrants for years in consulting work and I believe the proof is found in the practise.

These skills are equally applicable to your personal conflicts. If you have a child who won't do their homework, make the bed, or tidy their room without constant reminding and nagging, instead of going to Quadrant 1 where they are 'told', try moving the child to Quadrant 3 by way of pacing and leading interpersonal skills. These will create functional 'healthy' storming in Quadrant 2. Then adjust your relationship and task levels to influence the child into Quadrant 3.

A FINAL WORD

Perhaps the best way to see the link between assertion skills and managerial effectiveness is to realise the tools of influence are always about *power*. The choice is whether to use a *power-over* or a *power-with* style.

I believe the former does not give long-term benefits for either party. Co-operative problem solving is about assertive speaking and listening. The models of leadership quadrants and teamwork are frameworks on which to hang the interpersonal skills in a way that shares power.

6
Self-esteem

FOR THE PURPOSE of this chapter I define self-esteem as *how good we feel about ourselves*. Self-esteem is usually seen as our sense of confidence, well-being and happiness with ourselves.

I view self-esteem as the measure of our personal power. The term '**power-within**' is used throughout this book. It is meant to denote a sense of internal 'goodness' of spirit as opposed to compliance with external determinants of what is 'good'.

For some time the topic of self-esteem has been popular in workshops, training courses and 'pop' psychology books. In industry it is a topic that is often added to courses in managerial effectiveness, interpersonal skills and any program requiring personal growth or increased confidence. I have included a chapter on self-esteem for different reasons.

I am devoting a chapter to self-esteem because I view how we feel about ourselves as being critical to our capacity for personal empowerment which is, in turn, linked to our readiness and ability to communicate in a style of *power-with* others. In essence, I believe that communication in a *power-with* way is possible only for those of us who feel reassured that they have *power-within*.

WHERE DID OUR POWER-WITHIN GO?

During my work as a counsellor and teacher I have observed that most people appear to fear change. They tell me they are uncomfortable about changing their habits of communicating and are particularly fearful of the consequences of 'speaking up' with people who are significant in their home or work lives. Many worry about 'not being liked' if they confront someone.

I have been surprised at the numbers of people who truly believe that the way we are—the personality we are 'born with'—is largely how we will remain. A common view is that attempting to change one's own habits of behaviour is 'too hard' and even 'unnatural'.

It seems that personal growth or change is something most of us doubt we can successfully achieve. This very significant resource for personal power is somehow denied as an option for people in this culture.

Similarly, people doubt the capacity for social change. In fact, the majority of us do not even consider the possibilities.

Since beginning to teach management training and interpersonal skills from a social justice perspective, I have heard hundreds of course participants make statements indicating that the notion of changing an entire society or culture is either peculiar or crazy at best—at the least, an improbable chance. Certainly, the 'professionals' and managers report that they rarely if ever think or talk about such things as sex-role stereotypes, norms and societal conditioning. When I introduce the concept of unequal power relations in a society that condones oppression of many individuals and groups, some people look astonished and others say it is the 'nature' of human beings and 'you can't change the world anyway'.

I have often wondered about these phenomena, perceiving them to be a pervading theme of powerlessness at both a personal and political level. It seems to me that two common threads running through the people of this culture are impotence and low self-esteem.

It is my belief that this disempowerment can be traced to a socialisation process that somehow ensures we become what suits the 'power brokers' of the system and that we remain, from our earliest years, split-off from our instincts, spirit and *power-within*.

I firmly believe that ignorance, non-critical thinking and fear of recrimination are ways in which our culture maintains its lies and soul-damaging ways of keeping us separated from aspects of ourselves as well as from the potential connections we could forge with others. In this way, both *power-within* ourselves and *power-with* others in our relationships are made very difficult to achieve.

In Chapter 1, I linked win–lose habits and non-assertive communication style with the society of *power-over* and called this system our culture of patriarchal hegemony. I now add to this figure (Figure 6.1) *low self-esteem* (I am not okay, or I am okay because you are not) as part of our system's 'norm' of damaging any potential we have for *power-within*.

161

Figure 6.1: A model of power

POWER-OVER OTHERS	POWER-WITH OTHERS
(*Patriarchal hegemony*)	(*Sharing of power*)
Belief in absolutes	Acceptance/tolerance of different positions (beliefs and behaviours)
Sees 'Truths'	Realises ideas are within context
Values 'Right'/'Wrong' 'Correct'/'Normal'	Sees societal norms benefiting some and oppressing others
'The natural order' (it's the way things are)	Social injustice (society is contrived)
Hierarchies of power	├───────┤ Flatter structures
Legitimate power Win ↓ Lose	Referent (relationship power) Win ←→ Win
Competitive	Co-operative, collaborative
Trying to 'arrive' as correct	Just 'being' in the world
You are not okay — so I am or You are okay — so I am not	I am okay and You are okay
Estrangement, Disempowerment	Self-empowerment, Self-esteem
There's nothing I can do — 'it's not my problem'	A different future *and*, as well, a future of difference (where we celebrate difference)
Passive or Aggressive Communication	*Assertive Communication*
Power-over	*Power-with*

This chapter serves to integrate areas that our culture usually separates. I believe it is timely to consider how issues such as liking ourselves and speaking assertively—*power-within self* and *power-with others*—are connected.

CAN WE GET OUR POWER BACK?

I think so. I believe there is a wealth of resources both within each of us and in our potential connections with others and our environment that will enable us to create personal and political change.

For example, psychology has much to offer in assisting people to become their potential. In Chapter 1, I said that the *psychological* viewpoint is that we, as individuals, can grow and develop by exercising free choice and utilising skills that empower us in coping with our environment.

Teachers and counsellors in the helping professions use self-esteem enhancement as a tool to assist people to fight back against an oppressive, unfair social order or harsh upbringing. Group work, counselling and workshops reflect these views by focusing on recovery from damage done in childhood (or as an adult) by the family, church, school and other persons or institutions of the system. The process involves challenging many of the values and negative beliefs we have internalised from our cultural conditioning.

Many of the tenets of sociology sit comfortably with these techniques for regaining personal power. Back in Chapter 1, I said the *sociological* viewpoint is that people are limited in choices and skills because they have been indoctrinated by the significant people, rituals, norms and roles in their culture. While this group often concurs with much of the personal growth emphasis of psychologists, they tend to believe change at a personal level needs to be accompanied by more political action towards social reform. For example, most types of feminism advocate that we speak up about the injustices of our work, family and political institutions and insist that the power brokers take action to redress the inequities in these systems.

Some feminists work towards having improved representation from the so-called 'marginal groups' in each of the structures of our society. Others see lobbying the system as giving it more power and prefer to withdraw co-operation from some of the institutions of patriarchy. These more 'radical' feminists prefer to challenge the mainstream lifestyle as much as possible. Many live lives that involve non-conventional employment and work practices. Their relationships are often characterised by 'community' thinking and 'collective' spirit in working with others. At both ends of the feminist spectrum there is a theme of political activism as well as personal recovery and growth work.

There is a third group which offers its particular insights on the topic of self-esteem and reclaiming *power-within*. Amongst the terms used to describe these *spiritual* perspectives are 'new-age', 'sacred psychology', 'neo-pagan' and 'women's spirituality'. Each in its own way explores issues of our spiritual connectedness to the universe, the environment, and all living creatures past and present. These groups see our culture as lacking 'soul', as people are separated from their instinctive, spiritual health and power from within.

Workshops and books on these topics tend to involve

reclaiming our self-regard in ways that go beyond 'logical' and 'cognitive'. These forms of spirituality emphasise a 'self' which contains 'God' and goodness within as opposed to outside in a church or 'heaven' as is portrayed in mainstream religions. These alternatives focus on acting in ways consistent with your personal volition, while harming no one, and working for the good of all by remaining aware of the connections between all creatures of the universe and the sacredness in nature's cycles.

Some feminists see low self-esteem as arising out of patriarchy and its accompanying 'imperialist' forms of religion where we are cast as lowly sinners with God somewhere outside of us. The renewed interest in neo-pagan and women's spirituality rejects God as white and male and positions holiness and wisdom within each of us as we are part of the 'whole' of the cycle of creation, death and rebirth. This cycle is seen to encompass 'all' rather than elevate the value of a few.

There are other views that seem to encompass a combination of psychology, sociology and spirituality. To my mind, the work of Clarissa Pinkola Estés weaves something of all three perspectives. In *Women Who Run with the Wolves* she asks us to consider the ways in which most cultures damage, and even outlaw, the 'wild and healthy' nature of women. She talks of wounds that result when a woman's natural instincts are stripped away, and she suggests that the universal issue for women is learning to recognise how we are punished, frightened, and rewarded only when we agree not to see what is truly before our eyes. Estés urges 'revivification of our spirit' in ways that seem to combine the sacred, the political and the psychological.

For the remainder of this chapter, I will present the various positions on both 'cause' and 'solutions' from these various perspectives. On first inspection, some of the views of each do not always appear to fit comfortably with the others. I find that in the main, however, the theories and practices of each can be quite consistent with, or at least complementary to, the others. Personally, as I have explored my own self-esteem and reclaiming of power within, increasingly I have a sense of some kind of comfortable merging of my journey of personal growth, a desire for political activism and a thirst for spiritual attention and renewal.

You may find yourself more attracted to one view or set of skills than another. Different ideas and techniques appeal more or less at various stages of our life cycle. Alternatively, you may find a 'mix' of views and techniques to enhance your personal power makes more sense to you. If your personal journey has always been highly 'intellectual' you might be attracted to trying some of the more 'experiential' methods.

Pick and choose any of the self-help solutions from any of the three views presented, and get started on increasing your self-esteem—resurrecting your *power-within*.

A COMMON VIEW—THE 'PSYCHOLOGICAL' ONE

The most usual perspective on self-esteem comes from the 'human potential movement' where people are seen as being in the process of 'actualising' their potential. Emphasis for personal growth is placed on the person becoming more *inner directed* and taking charge of their destiny.

Popular psychology says that each of us needs to more fully 'own' our lives, stop blaming others and circumstances, let go of the need to justify or give up when things become difficult, and take on the 'adult' way of life. This means meeting our own needs by finding the inner resources to make our goals happen.

Industry training finds this approach appealing because it asks the individual employee to stop seeing problems as the company's or the system's, and to see solutions and faults as lying within each person. Solutions in industry include taking more responsibility for problems, time management, personal and professional goal setting and taking more initiative.

Most public workshops and seminars offered in Australia teach that enhanced happiness and effectiveness is found through taking greater responsibility for one's own life. Likewise, a lot of individual and couple's counselling is built around the notions of 'I am responsible for my actions—my achievements are largely due to what I have done in the past and can do in the future—I am what I think I am'.

The links between self-esteem and stress

Poor self-esteem can cause stress and even depression and anxiety. Stress is often defined as feeling out of control and unable to cope. It occurs when we don't have a strong enough sense of self and an inflated view of the capacity of people and things outside of ourselves to control us. The sense of *power-within* is withered in many of us.

One of the most significant factors contributing to stress and anxiety is *negative thinking*. People who think negative, frightening and what are often called 'irrational thoughts' cause themselves to feel depressed or panicky. This is not an unusual phenomenon attributed to small numbers of people who suffer some form of phobic reaction. On the contrary, many, even most, people think quite negatively about themselves or fearfully about various situations on a regular basis. Our culture seems to encourage this kind of thinking and actively discourages positive self-appraisal.

Learning to think more 'rationally' by challenging some of your beliefs and taking charge of your 'thought diet' will enable you to become whatever you choose to program in your own mind. Changing the way that you *feel*, as a consequence of deliberately changing the way you *think*, has a psychological term: 'cognitive behavioral restructuring'. It is often referred to as *positive thinking*. The details of how to do this are given in the next section entitled 'Solutions'. Learning to think more positively is the most popular technique found in personal growth psychology.

Solutions offered from the psychological perspective

These six techniques and sets of skills are generally accepted as crucial for self-esteem and reclaiming of personal power. Some authors and teachers who use this orientation say that if you incorporate any three of the following practices regularly you are unlikely to continue to experience stress or a diminished sense of personal power. Each of the techniques listed below is detailed further in specialist books, tapes, videos and courses.

1 *Changing negative thinking into positive thinking*

The idea here is that your thoughts don't just happen. You think them. You can control what runs through your head and can replace thoughts that upset you or hold back your abilities with those which will move you towards what you would like to achieve. Here are some strategies:

- 'Catch' yourself thinking negative or depressing thoughts. It takes practise. Most of us have been allowing ourselves to think like this for a long time. You may at first 'catch' yourself after you have been thinking irrationally. As soon as you feel depressed or anxious ask yourself 'What have I been thinking about?'

- Stop thinking those thoughts. You may notice that your mind goes back to that negative or depressing thought. Remind yourself that you are in charge of what you think and move your thinking onto another subject or do something different that occupies your mind.

- Change your negative thinking into positive thinking. For example, if you are thinking: 'I can't cope with being in small business. I should never have attempted this. What if there is no money to pay the monthly bills? What will people think? I'm hopeless at handling business situations. I can't cope . . .' *Change it*, but keep it realistic. Try this instead: 'I can't afford to worry unproductively like this. People who worry about daily bills never take business chances because all their energy is negative. I know that people are the sum total of their most predominant thoughts and because I'm thinking negatively and fearfully I'm going to take myself back into a second-class job when actually I *want* to make a go of my own small business. I can control my own thoughts and I need to focus on my goals as opposed to looking back over my shoulder and worrying about small details.'

There is a lot of information to suggest that we are whatever we think we are. Sport psychology works on these very principles in helping athletes to see themselves as playing 'perfect' shots and winning, as opposed as seeing themselves playing badly or coming second. There are many instances to back up claims that human beings can achieve virtually anything provided they believe that they can.

Affirmations are used by an increasing number of people every day. Affirmations are usually in the form of written positive scenarios that are read and imagined a number of times each day. For example, my affirmation may be 'I have a warm and supportive relationship with my son and every day we are getting closer and relating easily with each other'. If I really want this to happen (instead of arguing with my son much of the time) I need to picture this as a present reality and to keep rehearsing in my mind's eye what it looks and feels like.

Many business people carry affirmation cards with them with words such as: 'I work well under pressure. I stay calm and see conflict as an opportunity for me to display my skills and talents.'

As your unconscious mind cannot tell the difference between reality and imagination, affirmations help you program yourself as you would like to be. Your unconscious then believes that is how you really are, resulting in you moving steadily towards achieving that goal.

Affirmations are usually written in the present tense; for example, 'I *am* confident and relaxed' rather than 'I *will* be . . .' They tend to contain vivid descriptions to evoke positive feelings of succeeding. The technique is to *read* the affirmation, *picture* the scene in detail and *feel* what it is like for you to succeed in your goal.

Programming yourself takes some time (many people say about a fortnight of rehearsing the affirmation at least twice a day) but the more you affirm yourself as you would like to be, the more you will find yourself making decisions and taking actions that move you in that direction.

2 *Exercise*

Many stress management therapists believe that besides negative thinking the most common lifestyle similarity in stressful people is inadequate exercise. Physical activity is accepted as having positive benefits to self-esteem.

As a minimum, we need to do approximately thirty minutes of exercise three days a week, or twenty minutes five days a week and this needs to be of medium to high intensity aerobic work. Aerobic work of this kind involves having your heart rate up to 50 to 70 per cent of its maximum capacity.

If you plan to do only the minimum physical activity then you need to choose exercise that will achieve the right heart rate level in the required time frame. Suitable activities would include long distance walking (brisk), jogging, swimming, bike riding, squash and aerobics. Sports such as football, netball and tennis are partly aerobic and partly anaerobic, which means you need to do more than the minimum requirement each week. Playing sport and doing weights need to be in addition to the minimum requirement of aerobic work if your main consideration is enhancing self-esteem and reducing stress.

In a nutshell, exercise is vital. It tones your muscles, improves the cardiovascular system, relaxes your body and changes your brain chemistry to provide some natural highs.

3 Diet

The fundamental idea behind using diet to help enhance your self-esteem is that good eating habits give you a healthier, stronger body to combat life's stresses. Current recommendations are to develop an eating regime that cuts down on cholesterol, fats, sugar, salt and red meat and increases the intake of fruit, vegetables, wholegrain cereals, breads, pastas and water.

Unhealthy patterns of eating, including addictions to overeating and alcohol, are often symptoms of low self-esteem. For some people a sense of powerlessness leads to, or at least accompanies, their eating problems.

There are a multitude of books available on the topics of diet and good nutrition. Likewise, there are a number of courses now available on recovery programs for overcoming patterns of personal abuse including eating disorders.

4 *Goal setting*

Finding and achieving goals is a well-accepted practice to enhance a sense of personal power. Set yourself small and large, long-term, immediate or short-term goals and make them *written*, *specific* and *detailed* in the steps required to achieve success. Time limits need to be set to achieve goals and monitor and reward your progress. Even small achievements seem to develop immediate confidence and improved self-esteem.

It is important for you to get in touch with what you really want, need, wish for, or dream about before setting goals. This may be difficult for those of us who have been heavily socialised into fulfilling mainstream roles and norms. Before setting your goals it is useful to do some exercises clarifying your values and 'visioning' the possible changes to your emotional, mental, social, financial, career and home circumstances.

Many audio tapes and seminars are always available on the subject of goal setting.

5 *Communicate well with others*

Here are some useful keys to improved communication:

- Be honest with yourself and others. Get in touch with what you need and want and be prepared to say so. This includes confronting another person whose behaviour you're not happy with.
- Don't judge people. Respect and tolerate their differences from yourself. (This assumes that people realise there are different points of view on any issue and that each individual has a viewpoint developed as a consequence of their life experiences. An uncommon trait of people in our society is genuine

tolerance for and true understanding of differing views.)

- Own your own feelings and thoughts. Say 'I . . .' when you are expressing your opinions.
- Express your ideas and needs without ignoring or violating the other person's.

Chapters 2, 3 and 4 provide you with information on how to communicate well within relationships.

6 *Practise relaxation techniques*

Learn to relax *deeply* on a daily basis. Reading a book or listening to music relaxes you only moderately, and therefore these activities are not enough to rejuvenate your mental, emotional and spiritual capacities to the fullest. Deep relaxation methods of meditation, yoga, deep breathing, mental imaging and positive affirmations are significant ways to stay in touch with 'self' and improve personal or work performance. Deep relaxation allows the subconscious and creative coping part of you to operate and therefore gives you a better life *balance*.

Some of the latest audio tapes available for relaxing include guided imagery work where you are 'talked through' your affirmations and visions of how you wish to be.

ANOTHER VIEW—THE SOCIAL JUSTICE PERSPECTIVE

In this section I draw upon the views of some of the social reformists of our society—in particular, the positions taken by many feminists and people who often are called 'critical social scientists'. While the psychological view sees the individual as responsible for low self-esteem through thought and behaviour patterns, the social justice perspective sees poor self-esteem occurring as a consequence of the individual being denied '*power-within*' by systems and structures surrounding us from birth. In Chapter 1, I mentioned social justice issues and the sociologist's view of an unfair society—norms, values and sex-role stereotypes that act to constrain and damage our potential for feeling 'okay' about ourselves.

This view maintains that society influences us to believe that certain stereotypes, rituals and roles are 'normal' and that in reality most of the population does not fit in all or even many of the categories of 'okay'. As a consequence of these inequities, we are urged to challenge and change the way our culture is structured.

The 'way things are' is seen to be a distorted set of learnings that appear to come from respected information sources but which are really designed to keep some groups invisible and others invincible. In Chapter 1, I mentioned the categories of white, Anglo-Saxon, middle-class, middle-aged, male, heterosexual, formally educated, able bodied and so on as the 'dominant' groups in society. Until we raise our consciousness about these unfair practices of upholding some people as more 'correct' than others we are all terribly vulnerable to harmful undermining of our self-esteem.

In her book *Revolution from Within*, Gloria Steinem lists these 'lethal underminings' with regard to sexism as including:

> Being taught to revere 'the classics' of western civilisation, most of which patronise, distort, denigrate, or express hatred for the female half of the human race . . . surveying a tradition of art in which women are rarely artists and

often objects; studying biology that focuses more on human differences than on human possibilities; absorbing ethical standards that assume masculine values, and learning theologies that assume all male deities . . . being isolated from other women—perhaps resented by them—because we are educated like men.

In this example, I have chosen *sexism*. It is as easy to cite instances of racism, classism, scientism or heterosexism. The point is that what we learned as acceptable—and indeed normal—is an ideological distortion that is not serving our society equitably.

These hierarchical dynamics, where certain groups are superior and more privileged than others, set up win–lose situations. Competition perpetuates itself by suppressing the self-esteem of both the winners and the losers, making each constantly concerned about continuing to gain 'success'.

Even if you belong to most of the so-called desirable categories, you are likely to constantly strain to overcome fundamental doubts about your capabilities. This is because at some level, deep within your psyche, you know there are lies and myths in privilege. Those who happen to fall into most of the 'dominant' categories know they cannot seem to achieve the position of being the most 'correct' in this system.

Years ago, a cousin of mine on holiday in Australia from Britain remarked he had felt that the poor weavers in Indonesia were fundamentally more happy than he. This realisation disturbed him. How many of us have felt, with a soul-shattering moment of understanding, that our striving towards higher grades, more qualifications, or a societally condoned 'workaholism' will never provide the answers to the meaning of life? He, like so many people, went on to hope for solutions in another degree, promotion, and adherence to achievement of the norms of his British social order. What a terrible shame that we are encouraged to choose between 'bettering ourselves' and 'becoming ourselves' (Steinem 1992: 109).

Solutions offered from the social justice perspective

Most of the solutions that come from these perspectives are *social*, with emphasis on actions to gain a new kind of society. Some reformists believe social change will become possible only when we stop the new-age habits of self-absorption and looking *within* for answers. They worry that the psychological techniques offered in the previous section are an unhelpful focus. Other social activists advocate a combination of personal growth and political action to both shore up the individual and change the institutions.

1 *Deconstruction*

In Chapter 1, I mentioned a set of steps that enhance 'critical thinking'; that is, our ability to understand there are various realities for different people and that we are capable of having multiple positions simultaneously on any given issue (see Figure 6.2). For any position or behaviour that we advocate, there are people who are going to be advantaged or disadvantaged.

By learning to deconstruct so-called 'norms' and 'facts' of our culture, we provide ourselves with an *antidote* to win–lose thinking. Deconstruction prevents us from thinking simplistically and falling into habits of looking for the certainty which always involves some people winning and others losing.

Learning to use deconstructive habits of thinking yourself and asking other significant people in your life these kinds of questions can lead to increased tolerance and capacity for social change.

2 Raising consciousness

Social reformists contend that we need to raise people's awareness of the 'Lies, Secrets and Silences' (Rich 1980) of our social order. Courses and consciousness-raising groups are seen as critical to developing our ability to know what we don't know.

Towards this end, critical thinking is required and requested in our academic institutions, schools, churches and, of course, in the 'marginal' groups. In this way, the 'games' that are being played in our culture are named. Racism, sexism, homophobia, divisions of age, appearance, able-bodiedness, ethnicity and so on, are spoken about and given life. This is a strategy for unlearning definitions of humankind that have largely been the

Figure 6.2: Steps for deconstruction (critical thinking)

1 Identify all possible positions in the topic.
2 Where do you stand? And where else?
3 Where do your ideas come from?
  (Where historically have your ideas come from?)
4 Whose interests are served/not served by these positions? (Who's winning and who's losing?)
5 *Goal setting* — What do I now believe and why? Therefore what action will I take/not take?

178

efforts of the privileged few defining themselves as the norm and the ideal. This process attempts to ensure that so-called minority groups become included in education and the making of what has been called *knowledge*.

Some authors and teachers believe that we should become angry and 'fight back' against our oppression. Others say we should simply reaffirm our power in the face of oppression by changing our belief systems regardless of the commonly held conceptions. Gloria Steinem in *Revolution from Within* says:

> No matter who we are, the journey towards recovering the self-esteem that should have been our birthright follows similar steps: a first experience of seeing through our own eyes instead of through the eyes of others . . . telling what seems to be shameful secrets, and discovering they are neither shameful nor secret . . . giving names to problems that have been treated as normal and thus have no names . . . achieving empowerment in self government . . . bonding with others in shared power . . . and finally, achieving a balance of independence and interdependence, and taking one's place in a circle of true selves.

3   Raise consciousness and then lobby the system

It is common for reformists to claim that 'what we don't resist, persists unchecked'. The stance is to find unfairness unacceptable and to lobby the 'system' politically to demand change. For example, women, 'greenies', and indigenous people are being asked to become more powerful in the system by entering political and corporate life and to make a stand on policy issues.

This notion that we have a 'voice' and that we need to wake up and then speak up has had a significant part to play in the development of legislation and policy around issues of anti-discrimination, equal employment opportunity and social justice in our public service institutions.

4 *Raise consciousness and then* don't *lobby the system*
In some new-age, and even feminist, circles it has become more common to reject the idea of lobbying the system. Lobbying is seen as empowering that system because the people wanting change must 'ask' the dominant power brokers. The catch phrase here is the opposite of the one before—'what we resist, persists'. Sonia Johnson comments in *Wildfire* that we have been lobbying 'the boys' for about five thousand years and it is time for us to realise that it doesn't work.

This position is likely to advocate that you achieve a meaningful life yourself by ignoring many of the dominant, so-called 'truths' and find yourself marginal positions. For example, instead of working in corporate life where you have to deal with power broking, bureaucracies and patriarchal ways on a daily basis, consider your own business. The view here is that you are ultimately going to be healthier and more capable of changing people's views if you avoid mainstream politics and practices and live a more radical life. That is, if you are personally able to live a life that disturbs, provokes and challenges mainstream views and behaviours, you are actually creating reform within your own area of control. This is more empowering than asking power brokers for permission to change. Personal action is a political statement.

5 *Personal journeying*
If you browse through any bookshop in this country you

will notice a substantial section of books about 'recovery' from childhood abuse, 'co-dependency', addictions and internalised negative views of ourselves. I have noticed many workbooks use the word 'journey' in their title and are largely about nurturing and reclaiming the 'child within'.

I see courses on personal journeying as a combination of the psychology of growth as well as attention to notions of an abusive culture. Much of this strategy also encompasses a spiritual essence. This set of techniques is an example of how the psychological, sociological and spiritual can combine to offer a model and a series of practices to help people find their *power-within*.

An underlying assumption is that our poor self-esteem correlates with the abuse we may have suffered as children (or adults) when we have been treated harshly and have consequently come to believe that we are 'bad'. This continued self-hurt should be seen as a habit that we have picked up from the significant people around us and one that can be stopped. We *can* change the way we feel about and view ourselves.

While these programs vary somewhat in their approach to recovering a happy and healthy sense of self, a common theme is that it is possible to become for ourselves what we need to be by journeying back to the child we were. Recovery may be possible by experiencing what the child experienced, grieving properly for what we didn't have, and eventually becoming our own, much better parent.

There is no set path for people to reclaim a whole self from a damaged one. Some people use meditation and trance states to develop focused connection to inner

181

resources. Others prefer repetition of a mantra of some kind which calms and relaxes so the unconscious mind can surface and heal the 'self'. Others try more ancient yogic practices and hypnosis. All of these techniques are designed to reclaim unused parts of our self, heal damaged sections of our being and move towards a more satisfying and happy future. Reclaiming the 'inner child' often results in finding the creative, spontaneous, capable, loving and naturally confident person within us.

Sometimes, accessing the unconscious retrieves repressed trauma. This is believed by many to be a vital step to enable you to put a stop to old patterns and habits. There is much to suggest that many so-called 'bad habits' may be the telltale signs of buried abuse and trauma. Some examples of these symptoms include memory lapses from childhood, flashbacks of terror, eating, drinking and behaviour disorders, a 'Pollyanna' view of our own childhood, and difficulty in feeling or expressing emotions of past pain. If you are uncomfortable about embarking on this kind of a journey by yourself there are many therapists and counsellors who specialise in assisting adults overcome abuse from childhood.

Many of us now believe that a patriarchal social order does result in large numbers of people (perhaps even the majority of us) suffering as victims of a too-harsh upbringing and win–lose power dynamics in our primary relationships.

AN EMERGING VIEWPOINT—THE SPIRITUAL
PERSPECTIVE

There is a movement called 'spiritual' or 'sacred' psychology which is very popular in 'new-age' circles, therapy and personal growth courses. It is just beginning to be felt in mainstream human resource practice. This view sees God and sacredness as a presence alive *within* all people. The spiritual essence of a human being is found *within* the person, not *outside* in the structures and systems of mainstream organised religion.

Much of this spirituality celebrates seasonal cycles and the sacredness of the earth, and values all living beings as connected and equal. This can be seen in almost direct contrast to our anthropocentric view of the world (valuing humans as the most important creature on the planet) and our patriarchal culture which values masculine over feminine, church over humankind, humankind over the environment and so on.

New-age spirituality emphasises the healing properties in the cycles of seasons, moon, planets and in gemstones, crystals, natural remedies, magic, rituals and pagan traditions. *Women's spirituality* emphasises reclaiming religion from patriarchy. It has a more matrifocal essence, with the goddess, a symbol of a cosmic mother of birth, death, and rebirth cycles found within the earth, ourselves and our cycles.

From these points of view, self-esteem is very much a consequence of our spiritual belief system. If we believe that God and goodness are within us as in the pagan religions, then we feel good and confident about ourselves. If God exists outside of ourselves and we are unholy and even sinful, then we do not feel good about ourselves.

Studying these links between our self-esteem and spiritual needs is becoming very popular. People are searching for and finding meaning in these ancient spiritual principles and practices. Words like 'pagan' (which, like women's lore, has been negatively labelled in Christian times) are being reclaimed and restudied as rituals connected with their country of origin—'earth religions'. Connections are drawn between the person we are now and our forebears. Credence is given to notions of an instinct within each of us that has come from past spiritual lives or is inherited as a 'collective unconscious' from our ancestors' wisdom.

Power from within

Starhawk's *Dreaming the Dark* is a book which brings together the spiritual and political. Like many writers who link magic, politics and spirituality, she sees that the solution to our 'power-over' culture (patriarchy) is *power from within*. Much of her discourse is based on the old religions of the goddess, and a neo-paganism which comes from the pre-Judaeo Christian tribal religions.

In this type of spiritual discourse, our patriarchal civilisation is seen as something that drives 'a wedge between spirit and flesh, culture and nature, men and women'. This kind of rupture is seen as causing the various oppressions of race, sex, class and environmental destruction.

Patriarchy is seen as a system that splits us into parts. We are split from our environment, from the universe and from each other. Within ourselves we are split— spirit from mind, body from feelings.

Universal spirituality

Some movements go beyond reforming our existing organised religions and towards reclaiming or developing

Figure 6.3: A comparison between 'mainstream' and 'universal' religions

MAINSTREAM RELIGION	UNIVERSAL/WOMEN'S SPIRITUALITY
God is white, male	God is universal God is birth, death, rebirth cycles The goddess is mother of the cosmos and earth
God is in heaven, church, on the cross	God is within me
We are sinners	I am good, sacred in myself
'Pagan' is evil	Pagan is about country of origin and connections with cycles of earth, moon, healing, herbs etc.
Church over humankind Man over woman Humankind over fauna and flora	All of life is connected and sacred
Woman as temptress, unclean	Woman as sacred (the giver of life)

a *universal spirituality*. This resurrection of worship of all living things and acceptance of divinity within each of us is a reaction to the gap experienced between our spiritual self and our emotional/social/mental/physical being, as well as to our connections to the planet and all its creatures. Many people believe organised religion has interfered with our ability to be whole and to collaborate with each other and our environment (see Figure 6.3). As in much of our interpersonal relations, win–win (sharing power with others) is being sought and heralded as a true solution to the dilemma of our lives.

For Gloria Steinem, these notions were only 'inspiring possibilities' until in 1980 she took a boat trip down the Nile from the older parts of Egypt to 'younger' representations of our history. In *Revolution from Within* she describes the unfolding of history as she viewed the carvings, reliefs and excavations as she travelled down the river. The pictures clearly show the shift from the old pagan world where *all* of nature was holy, to religious imperialism and patriarchy.

As Steinem travelled the upper reaches of the Nile she found that older parts of the ancient world showed goddesses worshipped as a metaphor for creation and the cycles of life, birth, death and rebirth. All living things, male and female, were sacred and flourishing. Further down the Nile the stories depicted in the temples began to show themes of separation. Drawings showed sexuality and spirituality beginning to split apart. The goddess figures began to give birth only to sons who became larger than the females and eventually became rulers seated on the lap of a goddess who had become 'only a throne'. The great cosmic mother began to be shattered into separate parts and became goddesses of wisdom, moral judgment, fertility and so on.

By the fourteenth century BC, all religion was in the hands of male priests and kings. The darker skinned people were portrayed as inferior or not existing at all. In the centuries that followed, sacredness was withdrawn from all but a few males.

During the sixteenth and seventeenth centuries, Western society underwent massive changes. Starhawk says: 'It was a revolutionary time, but the persecutions helped to undermine the possibility of a revolution that would benefit women, the poor, and those without property.' Instead, the changes that occurred benefited the rising monied-professional classes, and made possible the ruthless, extensive, and irresponsible exploitation of women, working people and nature.

Many now believe that the persecution of witches (originally women and men who were poor, rural dwellers, healers or non-Christians) undermined the unity of the peasants and contributed to the deliberate fragmentation of society. Witches made convenient scapegoats. This was a time when people were faced with a sense of their own powerlessness in the circumstances of a changing social order, where the power brokers expropriated knowledge and land and took away from people a belief that godliness was within them and their time on this earth. The witch holocaust was part of a time when land (the means of subsistence) was taken from the peasants to enhance the growth of an economy based on money and ownership of both property and people. Knowledge was also exploited as a commodity—something to be sold only to those who could afford to get 'qualifications'.

The view is that spirituality at this time changed from a recognition of goodness and godliness in this world and this life to an elevation of belief in the afterlife, with its 'here and now' partners of individualism, competition and a Christian ideology of work for gain. These new doctrines legitimised *inequality* and material acquisition. *Ownership* became the new token of grace.

As to the current struggle for spiritual health, Starhawk concludes:

> Whether our immediate needs are for food, health-care, jobs, child-care, housing, or open spaces our ultimate

interest is the same—restoring a sense of the sacred to the world, and so restoring value to our own lives and to the community of beings—human, plant, and animal—that share life with us.

Steinem says that archaeological discoveries and carbon dating indicate that the system of patriarchy, including imperialism in religion and race, account for only about 5000–7000 years of the three and a half million years of human history. For most of the time that human beings have existed, they connected very differently from the way we do now. This suggests it *is* possible for change, whether it be a return to some of the older ways of connection, or to a whole new system that has not yet been fully envisaged.

Solutions offered from the spiritual perspective

Most of the practices offered from the new-age and women's spirituality perspectives involve various rituals and celebrations which use group energy and centre around birth, death and rebirth cycles of energy building and releasing. Some of the rituals involve the use of guided imageries, chants and songs from pagan times, and various practices of magic, the 'craft', 'wicker' and the old religious ceremonies of the goddess and witch-craft. These rituals tend to be joyous celebrations of our kinship with nature, past lives, seasons and cycles.

In most capital cities there are various spiritual heal-ing centres, retreats, and ashrams where yogis, gurus and other spiritual leaders offer guidance to those seeking spiritual renewal of these kinds.

There are numerous authors who state that women's culture, spiritual wisdom and 'love' have been written out of history. We can find out about women's rich history of intuition, healing and their spiritual connec tion to cycles of life–death–rebirth by reading 'herstory'. Books of herstory also speak to the silences surrounding women's oppression, annihilation and the ongoing damage to women's self-esteem in the structures and rituals of a patriarchal society.

So-called 'new-age' bookshops in most cities stock a number of books on women's spirituality, earth religions, sacred psychology and 'herstory'.

WHERE TO FROM HERE?

I began this book by relating that interpersonal communication skills or 'assertion', as they are commonly termed, come from someplace and lead to somewhere. From Chapter 1, I have termed win–win communication skills as '*power-with*'. The more usual habits of passive or aggressive communication, as I have indicated throughout the book, are really about '*power-over*' in its various forms.

Chapters 2 to 5 have detailed the practicalities of how to speak and listen with others in the more 'contemporary' manner of *sharing power* to solve problems. Chapters 1 and 6 have emphasised the connections between our habits of communication and the culture that has caused these practices and is capable of being changed by altered forms of communication.

I firmly believe that I enhance my own personal power by realising choices and acting in ways that are about being responsible for my own needs. I have experienced the enhanced self-esteem that comes as a result of using many of the techniques offered in this chapter under the headings of 'psychology' and 'personal growth'. Probably the most significant single tool I ever use for personal power is speaking assertively to people who are insisting on a win–lose outcome. I find the skills of pacing and leading (described in Chapter 4) nothing less than brilliant. It is very exciting to turn a conflict situation around into a 'power-with' collaborative result when the other person had every intention of 'beating' me.

I have experienced similar delight when listening to the account of someone who had recently learned how to 'DESC' (see Chapter 2) and used it the day before to great effect with someone significant in their home life or perhaps their boss. It gives me great pleasure to watch somebody's animation as they say with some incredulity: 'It worked, it really worked. He changed his attitude completely and we sorted it out.'

Then there are the managers who begin to use open questions and paraphrase for the first time with a diffi-cult staff member. Others begin to use the Quadrants of leadership as well as encompassing their new power-with interpersonal style. Their sense of achievement and personal power is high. Accompanying this is usually an account of how the staff member also seems 'much happier now' or appreciates the increased responsibility and choices being shared with them.

While I have tremendous belief in, and appreciation of the tools of personal empowerment found in commu-nication skills, I don't believe they stand alone as the key to reclaiming personal power. I believe their effec-tiveness is greatly enhanced when they are used in combination with other techniques such as those detailed in this chapter under the headings of 'spiritual' and 'feminist/sociological' viewpoints.

Chapter 6 serves as a reminder to the reader of the context of 'power-with' techniques of communicating and seeks to reconnect issues of *'power-within'* that our culture usually keeps separate.

If you were attracted to this book because you wanted to change the way that you related to other people, I hope you have become more aware of the connections between our interpersonal habits and our societal norms. I propose that you can shape a *different future*—both for yourself and as part of a critical mass of people who are changing the habits of a society.

I urge you to think again if you are still thinking that changing over to 'I statements' would be too hard, awkward and not 'my usual way of speaking'. Your habits of communication are contrived, and that means, with effort in another direction, they are completely changeable. If you have had a habit of losing to other people you can change your passive style to one that is assertive. If your pattern has been to try to beat others, you can adjust your interpersonal style to collaborate and share power to solve problems.

You can change the way that you speak and listen to other people, deal with conflict or influence people. By doing so, you can also disturb our culture.

For me these are compelling reasons to bother to learn new ways of communicating. During our time we are capable of making change at both a personal and political level. 'Power-with' interpersonal communication is a truly significant tool for doing both.